THOUSANDS
OF YEARS

SCRIBNERS SCIENTIFIC MEMOIRS

John A. Wilson

THOUSANDS
OF YEARS

An Archaeologist's Search

for Ancient Egypt

CHARLES SCRIBNER'S SONS

New York

To the memory of
my father and my mother

CONTENTS

ILLUSTRATIONS

(following page 104)

THOUSANDS
OF YEARS

INTRODUCTION

TURN OF THE TIDE

THERE were no signs and portents in the sky over Quaker Hill, New York, when I was born on a September day in 1899. No flaming star rushed from the Berkshire hills toward Egypt. No zodiacal light formed a pyramid in the heavens. Those ancient crones, "the seven Hathors," did not come to pronounce a destiny over an infant. The gods slept quietly while a baby was born in the manse.

But even though the gods ignored all babies born at the turn of the century, a world which was five thousand years old in its forms was changing with amazing rapidity. While the gods slept on Mount Olympus, men were remodeling the world around those babies, from wood and stone and brick to plastic and steel, from pen and ink and paper to typewriters and radios and computers, from kings and peasants to dictators and tractors, from complacency and plagues to neurosis and old age. We children grew up in a setting that had extended from the architect-physician Imhotep of Egypt, from the law-giver Hammurabi of Baby-

lonia, from the prophet Moses of Israel, and from the philosopher
Plato of Greece. We have become old in a setting that is still
changing under such influences as Marx and Gandhi and Einstein
and Henry Ford and Thomas J. Watson. We have witnessed the
Götterdämmerung, in which the computer has replaced the gods.
A rip tide has washed away our castles in the sand.

Many omens, threats, and promises appeared just before the
turn of the century. Louis Sullivan put up a building that was a
steel skeleton supporting terra cotta and glass; Roentgen discovered X rays; Freud published his first case studies; the Lumières
showed motion pictures; and Marconi sent out successful radio
signals. Henry Ford was making his first automobile, and the
Curies were separating out radium. In the first years of the twentieth century Queen Victoria died; the Orient became aware of
its sleeping potential when Japan defeated Russia; and Russian
workmen marched to the Winter Palace to make demands upon
the Czar. In those years the Wright brothers flew an airplane,
Einstein proposed a theory, and *les Fauves* exhibited a drastically
different art in Paris. We babies were born into one of the most
interesting times in world history.

Egyptology itself was changing in that year 1899. Just three
weeks after I was born, eleven columns in the great temple of
Amon at Karnak fell with a resounding crash. A modest program
of consolidating that monument was started. It would be seventy
years before a Franco-Egyptian Center at Karnak would be
formed, not simply to repair and replace, but to seek the underground and aboveground causes of decay. It was in 1898-99 that
Flinders Petrie excavated at Abadiyeh and Hu and worked out
a system of pottery analysis that finally put the prehistory of
Egypt into a sensible order. That was a major breakthrough.
Ludwig Borchardt published an article on some papyri, giving
an astronomical dating for the Twelfth Dynasty and bringing
an end—a slow, lingering end, to be sure—to some of the wilder
dates for the earlier dynasties.

Norman Davies, copying in the tombs of Sheikh Said and

Deir el-Gebrawi, set new standards of exactness in the recording of Egyptian monuments. It was now obvious that a scholar who made hasty copies in a notebook on the basis of two days at a site was unreliable. Griffith's publication, *Stories of the High Priests of Memphis,* showed that the difficult demotic script could yield consistent secrets to a man of genius or to those who followed genius. Demotic was the very cursive writing in Egypt from about 700 B.C. onward. Two brilliant young men, James H. Breasted and Alan H. Gardiner, joined the staff of the great hieroglyphic dictionary at Berlin, thus finding acceptance in the most productive circles for language. And Gaston Maspero returned to the directorship of the Antiquities Service in Cairo. This was a final assertion of the French command of Egyptology. Maspero was gifted enough to accept the collaboration of scholars from other countries and to bend to the first demands of Egyptian nationalism. In archaeology the new force was discipline, whether as teaching, order, or pressure. There had to be orderly control. Any year could be a turning point to some degree, but there were signs and portents in Egypt in 1899, even though they were unknown in New York State.

In the revolution that had just begun, both in our way of living and in the field of Egyptology, I was to play a supporting role to the heroics of star actors. What follows is my view of the drama as it has unfolded thus far.

ONE

HERITAGE

THERE was nothing in my family background that pointed toward ancient Egypt, and it would be twenty-two years before the fascination of Egypt captured me. On both sides of the family there were hard-working, middle-class American citizens, for whom the future and the United States offered ample opportunity. Although Bible reading at daily prayers made me aware that Joseph and Moses had been in some place called Egypt, that was only a little more real than "the land of Nod, on the east of Eden," or "the wilderness of Sin." I was a dreamer, but my dreams were parochial. A certain pessimism about my career was once voiced by a New England gardener, who said, "If that boy John makes his way in the world, he'll have to do it with his head." Tentatively I was slated to be a preacher or a teacher, both of which were in the family tradition.

My mother's ancestors, the Lanes, arrived in America in 1652. The family began with strong attachments to New England and the Congregational church. As time went on, the abolition of slavery and the Republican party became two other powerful devotions. The family did move west to Ohio, but a restless foot did not develop until my great-grandfather, Samuel Alanson Lane.

In the 1840s he was editor of the *Akron Buzzard*, and his editorials were pungent, even though couched in an outlandish vocabulary. When the "Blacklegs" of the opposition understood his language, they would beat him up on the street. He developed what the doctors called "a consumption" and was given only a short time to live. My brother, a specialist on tuberculosis, believes that Great-grandfather had ulcers, but that ailment was not within the purview of the physicians at the time. To fill the remaining months of his life, Great-grandfather in March 1850 joined a party that was going to California, on foot most of the way. He then lived for fifty-five more years, to the age of ninety. The family repeated with awe the story of that heroic trek, and we children would ask for episodes to be repeated for our wonderment.

There was the tale of the magic cheese. Lane had brought from Akron a fifty-five-pound cheese in a great round wooden box. From St. Joseph, Missouri, the wagon-train jolted westward for three weeks before the box was produced and a generous wedge of the delicacy added to the evening meal. The case was closed and put back into the wagon. After some days they became cheese-hungry again, retrieved the box, and opened it. There lay a perfect circle of cheese, with no wedge or seam visible. They cut out another big wedge, closed the case again, and put it back into the wagon. The next time they opened the box the cheese had once more become an unbroken circle. As the springless wagon jolted across the rough prairie, the cheese had settled down, accommodated itself to the roundness of the box, and closed its gap. "Lane's magic cheese" became a tale that lightened the weariness of slogging across prairie and mountain, of stumbling over rough ground, of sweltering in the midday sun and then standing sentry duty at night, and of the terrors of the brackish Humboldt Sink in Nevada.

Somewhere west of the Rockies the hard bread dislodged one of Lane's porcelain teeth, which had been fitted into his jaw in Akron. He mounted the tooth on a sliver of hickory wood, poised this contraption over the gap in his jaw, and drove it home with a horseshoeing hammer. It stayed in place for years. Three generations later that heroic blood seems to have become somewhat diluted.

It took five months to reach Sacramento. By August 1850 the fever of the gold rush had abated. The four mules, which had cost $360 in St. Louis, brought only $175 in California. Lane took a job as a painter in San Francisco, using a rough ten-by-twenty-foot shack for his office. The wooden slabs of this shanty projected at the corners, and mules came to scratch their backs on these spikes. Lane kept a wooden club near the door to chase them away. He still thought of himself as a newspaperman, and he was writing a report on a San Francisco fire for the *Akron Beacon* when the hut began to shake vigorously. He seized his club and ran outside. There was not a mule in sight. He went back inside, finished his story, and went off to mail it. Only then did he discover that he had missed the story of the day, a brief but vigorous earthquake.

In 1852 he returned east, crossing the Isthmus of Panama in a party of which more than thirty died of cholera. Within a few years he became editor-in-chief of *Akron Beacon* and probate judge of Summit County. In 1881 he was elected mayor of Akron. Within Mother's family he was the great and famous man.

My maternal grandfather, Julius S. Lane, was a mechanical and mining engineer, the inventor of a number of ingenious devices, such as the Lane Mine Hoist. His company to manufacture these hoists was wiped out in the panic of 1893, and he always blamed President Cleveland and "those Democrats." As a mining engineer he traveled extensively here and abroad. In South Africa two Americans participated in the Jameson Raid in 1895 and were captured by the Boers. Grandfather happened to be there on business at the time and was deputized to serve as consular agent on their behalf while they were held in the prison camp.

He and Grandmother Julia lived with our family in Brooklyn and Connecticut for eighteen years, so that we children were brought up by two generations. With his Yankee ingenuity, he was the family Mr. Fix-it, always figuring out some way to keep things going. He dressed with a certain formality, and in his waistcoat pocket he carried a small assortment of industrial diamonds. To small boys diamonds were diamonds, and we were properly impressed. At the age of seventy-eight, with no advance word to his family, Grandfather went out to an airfield on Long Island and hired a pilot to take him up for a flight in one of those flimsy 1919 planes, with a little stunting thrown in. He was a fascinating combination of religious and political conservatism, on the one hand, and technological mobility, on the other.

His wife Julia was also brought up on the Middle Border. Her father had been one of the founders of Western Reserve College in Ohio. Her maternal grandfather had had a station on the underground railway for runaway slaves in Ohio. Her mother remembered lying in bed with small black children hidden under the covers down at the foot, while the United States marshal searched the house. Grandmother's mother died while she was a girl, and she had to bring up her younger brothers and sisters. She had six children of her own, of whom my mother was the eldest girl.

Grandmother's genius was for family. While she lived—to the age of eighty-eight—we belonged to a huge clan of uncles and aunts and cousins, who dutifully served her matriarchate. On my father's side there was one uncle whom I never met, and I barely knew who my cousins were. But the maternal clan was bound together by a family letter, the "Lane-Pitkin Family Omnibus—Always Room for One More." Woe betide the household that did not add its own letter and forward the "Bus" to its next station! Most of my boyhood was spent at the ends of a seventy-mile-long axis running between Brooklyn, New York, and Sherman, Connecticut; but we were aware of a larger world because we had relatives as far away as Illinois.

My mother, Pauline Lane, was a quiet and gracious but resolute woman, who loved people and was not particularly interested in ideas. She received love in return. In 1892 she completed studies at Oberlin and became that relative rarity for the time, a woman college graduate. She met my father, Warren Wilson, at a college students' Christian Camp at Lake Geneva, Wisconsin, and the handsome young theologue was swept off his feet and proceeded to sweep her off her feet. It was not easy: his background was Pennsylvania Scotch-Irish instead of New Englandish Ohio; he was a Presbyterian instead of a Congregationalist; and his politics leaned toward populism instead of staunch Republicanism. As a minister, he was not orthodox: he had been called to the pastorate of a non-denominational church at a place called Quaker Hill, near Pawling, New York. In those days a community church was unaccountable. But Warren Wilson had charm. In 1894 he and Pauline Lane were married at Sweetbriar Farm in Westport, Connecticut, and took their honeymoon in a one-horse buggy on the way to the manse in Quaker Hill.

My father's family came from northern and Protestant Ireland. Their Black Irish moods and their attraction to the mystic were still present, but usually kept under careful wraps. In 1830 my great-grandfather came to Baltimore, from Cootehill near Dungannon in Ireland, and married the daughter of an Irish-American doctor. My grandfather, John S. Wilson, in his turn married an American of Scotch-Irish descent and moved to western Pennsylvania. He had eight children, of whom my father was the fourth. Grandfather went into the newly booming oil business around Oil City and Bradford. He was a small operator, and there were big operators and panics; he failed at least once, yet he never lost his faith in petroleum. He believed that crude oil was good, whether applied externally or taken internally; his fine red beard and head of hair were kept clean and shiny with oil. His wife died early, and he and his eldest daughter brought up two preachers, a businessman, a military officer, two schoolteachers, and a lawyer.

My father was born in 1867 and came to his schooling when times were lean. He had to work his way through school and college, and he was determined that no child of his should have that burden. He had wanted to go to Princeton, but family finances forbade that, so he went to Oberlin instead, and then to Union Theological Seminary in New York.

The Harlem Division of the New York Central Railroad pushed sixty-five miles north of Grand Central to a vacant spot, which was to serve the town of Pawling. An enterprising man by the name of Albert John Akin had a house dragged across the fields to serve as the Pawling station. Mr. Akin lived on higher ground, an outthrust of the Berkshires called Quaker Hill. There was a Friends Meeting House there, and a community which went back into pre-Revolutionary days. The area was becoming farmed out, but now the railroad made it a convenient two-hour trip from New York. The great sprawling Mizzentop Hotel and neighboring estates became a summer resort for the more elegant middle class. The village benefactor gave Akin Hall as a community center and a non-denominational church, to serve the residents and summer visitors. In 1894 Warren H. Wilson was called to be the first pastor of that church.

Within my father there was a strong streak of protest, constantly at war with his Presbyterian conformism. It was not easy for him to bow and scrape before the stately dowagers from the Mizzentop Hotel or to accept the inertia of the old residents. He was never a patient man. But there were seminal characters too. He had been brought up to believe that fiction was frivolous in this dour world and that Sunday must be restricted to serious matters only. One Sunday afternoon Miss Margaret Monahan, a wealthy spinster lady, introduced him to *Alice in Wonderland*, and he came back to the manse, stumbling across the stubbly fields of late winter, avidly reading the book as he came. To us children Miss Monahan seemed an awesome autocrat, but she encouraged the young pastor to listen to his heart as well as to canon law. In 1908 she took Father and Mother on a Mediterranean cruise; they visited Greece, Egypt, and the Holy Land, with a side excursion to ancestral places in Ireland. Father returned with a great lot of very turbid photographs, but they gave us children an idea that the fairy tales might be right, because there were places in the world quite different from ours.

Quaker Hill had other persons who touched the heart rather than the head. Father had to listen to one farmer's humorous stories without being able to return joke for joke. Finally, in self-defense, he memorized three funny anecdotes, hitched up the horse and buggy, drove to that farm, and entered into a competition with the farmer. The only audience was a rather shiftless hired man, and Father was always grateful to him, because his uncontrollable laughter after Father's third story broke up the contest. Father was learning about people, a subject Mother had always known to be primary.

I was born in the manse. I was named after my grandfather, John S. Wilson, a preaching uncle John A. Wilson, my uncle Albert Lane, and Albert John Akin. At first Mr. Akin's nieces had objected to having a child named after the old gentleman. When they were assured that there were other good name-givers, they must have been satisfied, because a dozen years later one of them left me a legacy of $10,000, which helped tremendously toward my education at a time when Father had three other children in school.

When I was a few weeks old we moved to Brooklyn. Father had accepted the pulpit of the Arlington Avenue Presbyterian Church, an unprepossessing structure located in an unprepossessing part of an unprepossessing city. Where we lived the lots were rapidly filling with individual frame houses; one block away the low walk-up tenements looked out on the noisy El. Probably there were no other college graduates in the church at first. That was shortly to come with the younger generation. Certainly Mother, as a woman graduate, continued to be exceptional for a long time.

Father shook the place up. He campaigned for a stone and brick church to replace the little frame building. He became a follower of Theodore Roosevelt and preached a modified progressivism. He was much attracted by the revelations of Jacob Riis about the slums and by the social gospel as preached by Walter Rauschenbusch. Labor unions were fighting an uphill battle, and Father became chaplain to a union. He was insistent that every piece printed for the church should carry the union label.

Father believed that scholarly analysis should be a first step toward curing the world's evils. A Danish-born parishioner, Jens F. Bidstrup, encouraged him—almost forced him—to enroll for graduate study at Columbia University. Father's golf must have declined sharply when he had to give up that relaxation in order to take the two-hour trip by El and subway to study under a pioneer in sociology, Franklin H. Giddings. His dissertation was about the community of Quaker Hill as a social structure, and he gained his Ph.D. in 1908. If many in his church did not understand what he was studying, they were still proud of a minister who was energetic and scholarly.

In that perennial argument whether salvation depended upon faith or good works, the Presbyterian church felt that it should give more attention to mission work within the United States. Soon after Father had earned his doctorate he was called to head the Church and Country Life Department of the Board of Home Missions of the Presbyterian Church in the U. S. A. The office was in Manhattan, but we went on living in Brooklyn and attending the same church, which was a mistake. A pastor who had been influential in the life and character of a church should not have remained in the community when he ended his service, particularly if he left his successor with a mortgage to pay off on a new church. That was a lesson I understood at the time, yet later when I left administration, I could not act upon this knowledge. Where could a working Egyptologist have gone in those days? I therefore remained at the University of Chicago.

As a home missionary Father began the life of a traveling salesman; he was on the road for at least half of every year. He went wherever rural churches might need help: Ohio, Kentucky, North Carolina, Missouri, Kansas. He became endlessly weary of Pullman cars and railroad stations, of killing time in a dingy downtown area until the next train left. He did love his visits to the southern mountains. There was a trade high school in a lovely setting in Swannanoa, North Carolina, which he delighted to encourage toward a fuller program. It did advance, offering a rich opportunity to the young people of those hills, and after his death it was named Warren Wilson College.

Some in the church refused to accept the social gospel. Once a year the Presbyterian General Assembly would meet and face a proposal that all this work on rural churches and rural schools should be dropped. For a time we faced an annual crisis, but there were always enough delegates who felt that, if foreign missions were acceptable, home missions were also in place. The work kept on.

In 1914 Father began to teach rural sociology at Teachers College of Columbia University, adding a second salary so that his children might have a higher education without financial worry. A dozen years later he was teaching in the same field at Union Theological Seminary. He also learned something about the world abroad. In 1918, after the fighting had ended in Europe, he went to Germany to do educational work with the Army of Occupation. And he had two years in India, 1930 and 1931, for a survey of the Christian Mass Movement.

Father was a prophet of mixed gloom and hope. Thirty years before the rest of us began to worry about urban problems, he saw the modern city as an unnatural monstrosity, the advance of the machine as a menace to human dignity. He called upon man to recognize and reaffirm his community with animals and plants. He had an almost mystic belief that such an affirmation would restore man's religious faith. He once used an invitation to preach as the occasion for a parable about a man called Beelzebub, "the Lord of Flies," who had cornered the world market in fertilizer and thus controlled all food production. Men everywhere were enslaved to work for his enterprises. Finally, when Beelzebub's airplane was forced down in a remote valley, a great black bull, "the Lord of Dung," attacked and killed the soulless tyrant. The lesson was that ultimately nature will defeat the ruthless machine from the inhuman city. Our family loved the sermon. Unfortunately Father preached it in the beautiful colonial church in Litchfield, Connecticut, to an audience consisting mostly of retired city people. Not only had they no real interest in man as an integral part of nature, but they were not accustomed to hearing the word "dung" from the pulpit. After the service they left the church hastily and with ill-concealed indignation. All the way home Father pounded on the steering wheel of the car and cursed himself for a fool. His folly had been to raise a prophetic voice in so lofty a wilderness.

Good fortune in place and time has always been my lot. The first good luck was to be born into a family that was interesting and that could generate interest. Father's motto was "I Want to Know," and that fitted most of the family in one way or another. We knew that we lived in a world of unlimited fascination and opportunity.

⚜⚜⚜⚜⚜⚜⚜

TWO

BOYHOOD

For nine months of every year we lived in the drabness of
Brooklyn, creeping unwillingly to school, attending church,
Sunday School, and Christian Endeavor, and playing on the city
streets. We boys were dressed in shirts and ties, jackets and
knee-pants, long woolen underwear and long black stockings,
high black shoes that were latched by a buttonhook, and cloth
caps with visors that soon cracked across the middle. Then for
three months of the year we lived in a Connecticut paradise of
fields and woods and hills and ponds. There we wore only three
items—overalls, a shirt, and underpants. We were free. My
brother and I have found that we can remember much more
vividly the events of summer vacation than the round of restricted opportunities in the other three seasons.

There were four children, not too far apart in age—Margaret,
Julius, myself, and Agnes. We lived in a row of frame houses so
much alike that our house key fit any other along the block. Our
maternal grandparents lived with us, making a family of eight.

We were served by a succession of Norwegian sisters, who came over to the United States, learned the English language and American ways under Mother and Grandmother, and then went on to higher wages or to matrimony about the time that the next sister was old enough to come over. The kitchen needed many strong hands.

Feeding nine persons on a minister's salary imposed many problems on my mother. The impression that we lived on corn-meal mush, dried beef gravy, and bread pudding is surely not correct, but there was rarely a meat dish, and almost all of the cooking and baking was done at home. A small boy was always being sent out to the corner grocery for another cake of yeast or some baking powder. Oranges and bananas were rarities, but every autumn we brought back from Connecticut barrels of apples, boxes of fruit preserves, and sacks of potatoes. There was always plenty to eat and lots of milk, even though the variety of food was limited by a low budget and inadequate refrigeration. Insofar as we could get them, we wore hand-me-downs, usually from well-to-do parishioners' families. We conformed to the practice of the day by rinsing face and hands two or three times a day and taking a bath only on Saturday evenings.

There was good reading for a boy or girl because the Carnegie Free Library was only two blocks away. At the age of twelve I went through all the books of Jules Verne in about three months. Mother read Scott, Dickens, and Victor Hugo to us, and occasionally we had the treat of Father's reading a short story or some of Robert Burns's poetry. We always understood what Mother read, and we were excited by the gusto of Father's reading even when we might not quite understand it.

A Presbyterian home saw no Sunday papers, and we were allowed to play only Bible games on that day. We were not permitted to see the primitive motion pictures or to go to vaudeville. The theater in general was out of bounds, but we could go to the circus at the Hippodrome, see the Scottish comedian Harry Lauder on his annual visit, and once had the tremendous experience of seeing Montgomery and Stone in *The Wonderful Wizard of Oz.* However, once a year Uncle Howard Wilson would leave his church in Pennsylvania and come to New York for a refreshing round of theatergoing. The next day he would tell us the plot of the play or sing us songs from a minstrel show, such as "Everybody Works but Father" and "An Elephant on His Hands." We did not lack for entertainment.

Public School 108 was only a block away, a cold and gloomy pile of brick, with long, smelly corridors. The teachers were earnest spinsters, whom we called impartially "Old Lady Larkin" or "Old Lady Pratt," without any reference to their ages. Most of the children came from the families of clerks or factory workmen, but we were near enough to the slums so that there was a high percentage of recent immigrants from Italy or Eastern Europe. Many of these children were sewn into their woolen underwear in the autumn and not released from that warming armor until late spring. The first two years were coeducational; after that the classes of boys and girls were separate. From the age of eight until I was myself the teacher, I was not in a classroom with girls. In that respect my education was limited.

Children in Brooklyn at the beginning of the century wanted to learn and get ahead in the world. Problems of discipline were minor. The minister's children had such home advantages that we could forge ahead of our contemporaries and be advanced to higher grades, so we finished elementary school rather young.

The monotony of schooldays was broken up by a ritual of high days and holidays. Halloween and April Fools' Day had their ceremonial of pranks—marking other boys with chalk or smiting them with a stocking loaded with flour or pinning the sign "Kick Me" to somebody's coattails. Election Day was a great time. For a month before, we boys would appropriate barrels or wooden boxes and store them away under our back porch. On the evening of Election Day we would drag all this out into the middle of the street in front of our house and have a big victory bonfire. It did not matter to us which party won;

we used the occasion for a monstrous celebration. As long as the street was paved with cobblestones, the police watched this exercise tolerantly. But the year that the street was asphalted the fire engines had to be summoned twice to put out our fire.

A generation later in Chicago, children went out for their "Tricks or Treats" on Halloween, but in Brooklyn we did that on Thanksgiving Day, going from door to door in homemade masks and begging for handouts. The great festival of the year was Christmas, beginning with its ritual of stockings before dawn. We children could not wait until it was really light, and our premature excitement often displeased our overworked father. Breakfast and family prayers on that day seemed interminable, but finally there came the ceremonial of the Christmas tree with its incredible mound of presents. The tree was decorated with candles, so that there had to be a bucket of water at hand in the parlor to put out any sudden fire. If financial stringency limited what we might give or get, we were the more delighted with the bounty that was possible.

At the age of ten or eleven I made my first public speech. The Sunday School had sent Thanksgiving baskets to an orphanage. On the following Sunday I stood up before the assembled seventy or eighty faces, mentally closed my eyes to them, and concentrated on the speech I had memorized so carefully. "Last Wednesday the committee took the baskets over to the orphanage. As we came in the front door we were struck by several things." I probably wanted to comment on the sparse order of the place, but I paused at this point to review the next sentence in my mind, and some quick-witted boy down in the front row snickered. So I conscientiously went back to revise the previous sentence: "What I mean is that there were many things about the place which struck us right away." That gave the slower-witted youngsters a second chance to get the picture of visitors being bombarded, and there was a burst of laughter. I cannot remember whether that speech was ever finished. But for the next sixty years I anxiously went over the first sentences of any public speech.

My brother Julie was two years older than I and also twice as enterprising. He had friends of his own age, and I tagged along, trying to keep up with their games or their sophistication. We quarreled endlessly, as brothers will, but I followed him with doglike devotion, and he was always generous enough to let me join in his pastimes. If we thought that "the Fulton Street Gang" was going to attack us—I do not remember that they ever bothered about us, but the threat was always there—we were united in a firm front against the enemy. We played "catch" or "cops and robbers," built wooden shacks in the back yard, or went sledding on a nearby hill. Rainy days were dreary: we had to stay indoors and play "house" with our sisters.

At the end of June five adults, four children, and probably a dog would leave the city house, carrying a monstrous variety of suitcases and packages, board the El and then the subway, to make the two-hour trip to Grand Central Station in Manhattan. Then there would be a two-hour ride on the Harlem Division railroad to Pawling. The weather would be hot and sticky; we children would be overexcited and exhausted with anticipation, so that we always had to rush out to the open platform to be train-sick. At Pawling, George Durgy would meet us with a team for the two-hour drive across the hills to his farm in Sherman, Connecticut.

Father had met Durgy when he had served as visiting preacher for the little Coburn Meetinghouse in Sherman. And it was to Durgy's big, hospitable house, Valley Breeze Farm, that Father packed the family off on the first hot, humid day. The first time I went I was ten months old. We rented half of the house for five dollars a week per adult and one dollar a week for each of the two older children, and "we'll throw in John for his smile." We had three happy summers there.

Next to Valley Breeze Farm was the big Wanzer farmhouse. The last of the Wanzers had become incompetent, and the selectmen of the town had moved an indigent and shiftless family in to take care of him. When he died, this family got the house and the twenty-three acres of land that went with it. George

Durgy and Jens Bidstrup urged Father to buy this property. All his life Father had had a horror of debt, but they pushed him through the deal, including its black cloud of mortgage. Later he sold five acres to a Brooklyn doctor for enough to retire the debt. Waterside, named after an ancestral place in Ireland, was ours. Now we really had a home.

The farmhouse stood high above the dirt road winding through the valley. The downstairs rooms were huge; the kitchen had ten doors. The upstairs rooms were either immense or tiny. Once I slept with a neighbor boy in one of the smallest rooms. During the night I must have been pushed out of the narrow bed, because I awoke to find myself nested in a bureau drawer. Our family broke through the partition that had once divided the family bedrooms in front from those of the hired hands in back. Fireplaces and wood stoves provided heat. We piped water into the house, but for twenty years we used only the outside toilet, screened by hollyhocks and a trellis carrying trumpet creeper. Some of the house was already well over a hundred years old, but the timbers were excellent. A place like that takes a never-ending hold upon the affections.

Warren Wilson wanted others to share this little paradise. Some of his Brooklyn parishioners came and looked. Soon there was a summer colony of eight or more city families, stretching for a mile along the narrow, hilly, dusty road, past the cemetery and the glen and Mr. Bidstrup's Overlook, to Leach's Corners. Most of the families had children near our age. Mothers and children would spend the summer there. Fathers would come up for weekends and their two-week vacations. There were Saturday picnics in the grove, hayrides, fireworks on the Fourth of July, the annual church donation, and the annual clambake and gun shoot. Every few years Father would organize a play or a historical pageant. On August 1, 1914, while Europe was collapsing into war, there was a play to raise money to put a roof over the boathouse.

The gentle trough of land in front of our house had a sluggish stream and was too swampy to be good farming land or pasturage. George Durgy and Father conceived the idea of turning this into a placid little lake. They organized an association and sold shares of stock. The money was never quite enough, but a dam was built and the lake filled by the spring of 1908. Father named it Lake Mauweehoo after the last Indian chief of the area. It was a name that fitted nicely into the mouths of kids on a hayride; as they passed a farmhouse they would shout, "Who? Who? Mauweehoo; Mauwee . . . Mauwee . . . Mauweehoo!" Community life centered on the lake, with its boathouse and ultimately its clubhouse.

Every day culminated in a long afternoon swim. Before there was a Lake Mauweehoo, we went to muddy little Pepper's Pond. But the Pepper daughter objected to our swimming in the nude —she had to go up to a third-story window to verify that—so we made the two-mile trip to Mill Pond, which had not only mud but also bloodsuckers. So it was better to have our own lake, with our own boats and a raft as a goal for the bold swimmers. Horse-and-buggy distance away was beautiful little Green Pond, where we might have the excitement of camping out in the woods. Boys did not go into raptures, but we came to appreciate what wonders were made for us by water.

Within the colony there was a comic assortment of old horses good for no other purpose than summer folk. We had a buggy horse named Elijah Dowie, who had once been an unsuccessful pacer and now was as stubborn as his laziness would permit. In his last incarnation, as a lap-robe for the motorcar, Elijah was much more reliable than he had ever been in life. My sister Margaret had a riding horse, a western pony named the Merry Widow, who knew all of the tricks to use against a timid, inexperienced rider. Just as you were ready to mount her she would do a little dance. At a crossroads she would set her teeth into the bit and try to take the wrong road. Then, as you tried to saw her head toward the desired road, she would suddenly respond to the bridle, turn all the way around, and set off briskly for home. Father was experienced enough to handle these beasts, but they knew that they could intimidate the rest of us.

The first motorcar came in 1914 when Father bought a Model-T Ford. Riding along the narrow dirt roads, with their sudden turns and steep pitches, slashed by thank-you-ma'ams for drainage, was a breath-taking adventure. Could we make it up the steep Leach Hollow hill on the first run? If we had to back down again, where was the first place to pause and collect resources for a second try? The weekend was always a busy time of collecting fathers at the station on Friday evening and returning them on Monday morning. In one day Julie had to drive one hundred and four miles! People marveled at his heroic achievement and the durability of the car.

As in the city, we rarely had a meat dish as the center of a meal. There were more eggs than in the city, and we had fish from the lake, dried beef gravy, corn-meal mush, cottage cheese, all forms of baked goods, and good fresh vegetables from the garden or apples from the orchard. On Sundays we had chicken, and a maple mousse went into the ice-cream freezer before we started out on the four-mile ride to church; it would be ready when we came back. Fresh milk was four cents a quart, there were second helpings of everything, and the cookie jar was always available between meals. Mother said that she had a "leaky cookie jar," because we would head straight for the pantry with wet feet after swimming.

This idyll was broken by World War I. There were now more serious things to do than to dream in a boat on a placid lake. Julie went off to the service, ultimately into Naval Aviation. He and Grandfather had always done the handy work around the house, so that my natural clumsiness had been reinforced by lack of practice. Now I had to do the driving of a bulky old Haynes motorcar. The car's defective wiring would fail me, not before a trip started, but a mile away from home. This only confirmed my instinctive fears of machinery. The farmer who had inherited the Durgy place now had no hired man and was forced to accept my help. I did not even know how to twist my fork in pitching hay. Those two summers were good for me: I found that I could do things when I had to.

Today there is a broad motor road in front of Waterside. Cars take the curve just beyond the house at fifty miles an hour. The country store at Sherman Center is no longer a community meeting place; housewives can drive a dozen miles to New Milford or Danbury for shopping. Or they can run into New York and be back early in the afternoon. Cocktails before dinner are expected—or at any other time that seems convenient.

As Sherman has become a secondary suburb, literary and art people have been attracted to these hills. In the thirties, about the time of the Spanish Civil War, it was even whispered that there were Communists in this Eden. It may no longer be a retreat, but is still beautiful.

THREE

EDUCATION

My career was a problem. It was obvious that I would not be a success in the worldly sense. It might be best to look toward the ministry. Although my heart had heard no call, I tended to agree. In that case there would be a focus on the Bible, with a classical education, including Latin, Greek, and Hebrew. Words and word puzzles always attracted me, and strange languages might meet that pleasure. Picture writing as it appeared in the newspapers in cartoons or comic strips caught my imagination. At the age of twelve I was already doing some research by poring over baseball statistics and figuring out what major league players were best at sacrifice hits or double plays. When we parsed sentences in elementary school I delighted in the pattern of language. I was informed—incorrectly—that the principal parts of a certain Hebrew verb were: "kit-tail, cattail, coattail," and that seemed worth exploring.

Since Boys High School was one of the few schools in Brooklyn that still offered Latin and Greek I enrolled there. (Princeton was a warm possibility for college, and that university still required Greek for the B.A. degree.) I started Latin in my first year, and in my second year I offered myself for Greek, but I was informed that Greek was being discontinued because of insufficient interest. Thomas F. Flint, who had taught it, discussed this with me. When I expressed my disappointment, he offered to see me once or twice after class to tell me something about Greek, so that I would not lose interest before I got to college. I went to his room at the end of the schoolday, and he gave an enthusiastic lecture about a great language and its influence on literature and thought. He had some examples of Greek words that had lasted on into English, among them "acrobat" and "acropolis." "Now," he said, "*acropolis* means 'high city.' The first part, *akros, akra, akron* means 'high.' There is a city out west named Akron. Do you suppose that it is high?" I remembered Great-grandfather's big book, *Fifty Years and Over. Akron and Summit County*, and I answered promptly, "Yes, sir. Akron is in Summit County, Ohio." He looked at me in astonishment, turned, hurried out into the corridor, and stopped the first teacher to come along. "I have a boy in there who knows the counties in the United States!" he said in excitement. "He just told me that Akron was in Summit County, Ohio!"

The result was that Mr. Flint gave me three years of personal instruction in Greek, out of hours and without pay. I had him for Latin too. He was not a very good teacher. The boys terrified him so much that he was unable to communicate successfully. But he and I got along beautifully. He loved Greek, and he lost any fear of me when I responded by loving it also. The recurrent geometry of Greek tenses and cases delighted me, and the pleasure in grammar and syntax extended itself to a pleasure in literature. Father got me a Greek spool for his old Blickensderfer typewriter so that I could type out my lessons neatly.

At that time Boys High School was a cramming school for the state regents examinations. It had a brilliant record for pushing boys into scholarships at colleges in New York State. The general pattern was to stick to the textbook, because that would give the answers to the regents examination questions. But there was one teacher of history, Sidney D. Brummer, Ph.D., who went annoyingly outside of the pattern. If he asked a question about the Franco-Prussian War we would parrot back what the book gave as the answer. "All right," he would say, "and what do you think?" What did *we* think? Why should we *think* when the book had it all down in black and white? Most of us claimed that we hated him, but we respected him, so that we cautiously tried to say something of our own. At home I heard the give-and-take of argument at dinner table. Father had been a disciple of Theodore Roosevelt and then had shifted to Woodrow Wilson, whereas Grandfather had remained loyal to Taft. I knew that there might be difference of opinion, but I had not thought that this would extend to the authority of textbooks. Mr. Brummer was the first teacher to suggest that a boy might have a mind of his own and that education might include a little healthy skepticism.

There were two thousand students at Boys High School, of whom three out of four were Jewish. They had excellent minds, and competition in class was stimulating. I had no particular feeling for or against Jews. I was a Scotch-Irish Presbyterian, and I knew that there were others, Baptists, Catholics, Christian Scientists, and Jews, just as there were Germans, Italians, and Poles. Inevitably I worked and played with Jews. Every day I took the long trip to school with Milton Salomon. Benny Greenspan was one of the most humorously attractive characters of my acquaintance. The world was widened by knowing Sherman, who could ruin any teacher's joke by braying like a donkey, and Spike Newman, who earned his title by the distance and accuracy of his spitting. Only much later did I learn that Icky Newman had been so nicknamed because there was an Egyptian weasel called the ichneumon, but he endeared himself to me because when a teacher shouted at him, "Don't you hear what I am saying?" he was impelled to say, "Yes, sir, curiously enough."

It was not until my last year in high school that I came face to face with prejudice—in reverse. I was asked to be a candidate for class office on a ticket that offered two Jews and one other Gentile besides myself. It was called the Anti-Race-Prejudice party, which meant no prejudice against the Gentiles. We did not win, but it gave me a sense of what it means to belong to the minority. I became aware that I had been passed over for clubs or for favored positions. That did not worry me; I thought that the majority had a right to do what it pleased. Protest against absolutism would come to me only later in life. I have always denied that I had any racial or religious prejudice myself, but it is true that I have an extreme distaste for extremism in others.

Going from Boys High to Princeton University was like stepping out of a crowded streetcar into a limousine. Some of the passengers in the limousine were out for the ride only. They did not care particularly where the car went. Thus there was some compulsion on those who expected to reach some destination to accept the pace of the vehicle. There were very good departments in Princeton in 1916, and some excellent teachers, but generally speaking the "greasy grind," who strove for achievement in class, was looked down upon. It was still an educational resort for gentlemen, who could choose their classes and coast through with a minimum of effort.

The choice of Princeton was not difficult. Father had wanted to go there, and Julie was already there, pointing toward his premedical courses. It was famed for its classical studies. I no longer planned to become a minister; history and languages had now captured my interest. But perhaps I have remained something of a preacher all my life.

It was decidedly a dislocation for a preacher's son to move from provincial Brooklyn and rustic Sherman to sophisticated Princeton. In the first class parade I was next to a baby-faced contemporary who was guzzling whiskey from a flask. There was a gang of sophomore terrorists who tormented freshmen unmercifully. Fortunately my room was on the fifth floor, which was too high for their alcoholic adventuring. Once in my life I had traveled as far away from home as western Pennsylvania. Now my classmates came from all over the world. We were to produce a justice of the Supreme Court, a deputy secretary of Defense, a dean of the Harvard Law School, directors of banks, skilled engineers, and distinguished scholars. I was a downy chick thrown into a flock of cackling geese. Classmates talked carelessly about girls, whom I still held to be on a high spiritual plane. Fortunately my family setting had given me values I could not discard. Fortunately there were classmates who shared my innocence and my values. But my education was extended.

There was, for example, the exquisite who had lived in Europe and could discourse learnedly on art and music. With him and others, I went to New York and stood in line for the opera; once we heard Geraldine Farrar in *La Nozze di Figaro* and Enrico Caruso in *Aida* on the same day. I came to understand something about aesthetics. That was a short-lived acquaintance, but I gained new insights and somehow saved myself from going arty.

Ultimately I was drawn to classmates who had scholarly interests. Three in particular were good to me and good for me— Rensselaer W. Lee, Richard Hartshorne, and George M. Harper, Jr., known as "Mac." On the surface our friendship was jocular and colloquial. I kept a running record of the extracurricular antics of this self-styled "Quaint Quartet." But we all shared the same underlying serious purpose, and we stimulated one another. It has been the kind of friendship that can be picked up easily and warmly at any time. Then there was always my busy brother Julie to counsel me when I asked for advice. Princeton offered pleasures out of classes, and one could also find pleasures in class.

I walked through the majority of my courses without great interest. But Edwin Grant Conklin in biology gave us an exciting impression of the complex miracle of evolution. Otherwise the best courses were in classics and history, giving the bent to my career. Edward Capps gave us a superb course in Greek comedy, with a gusto that brought Aristophanes into the room, chuckling along with the rest of us. Dana Munro's medieval history was relatively impersonal, but he led us back to the basic source materials instead of relying on later interpretations. Walter Phelps ("Buzzer") Hall led us personally by hand through the intricacies of nineteenth-century Europe. Because my mind clung lovingly to such names as Pobedonostev and George Petrovich Karageorge, Buzzer gained too high an appreciation of my scholarship. When I failed by a few percentage points to make Phi Beta Kappa, he embarrassed me by trying to lobby me into that honor. Fortunately this was without success, because I had not earned it.

To Clifton Rumery ("Beppo") Hall in history I owe a great debt. The First World War invaded our college years, and I spent a few months in army uniform, expecting to go to Europe and defeat the Germans with great feats of derring-do. We were all so keyed up that the Armistice came as a great let-down. When I returned to classes I wasted my resources in frivolous purposes, as did the majority of my classmates. Mid-semester came, and Beppo gave me a third group. The Princeton grading system used first group in place of an A, second for B, third for C, and so on. I was annoyed but was still not focused on my work. One day after class Beppo called me to his desk and said briskly, "Mr. Wilson, I had you spotted as a first group student. You have been doing second group work for me, so I gave you a third group. That is all." I was furious. I made up my mind to show that tyrant. I buckled down to serious work and was a real student for the last year and a half. He was a good psychologist, and he gave me the needle at the right time.

My family environment, a natural Puritanism, the discipline of high school, and a relish for new information stood me in good stead. I had certainly been a naïve boy when I entered Princeton. The four years there enlarged my horizon, but I left there still a naïve young man.

FOUR

BEIRUT

Now my future had narrowed down to the teaching of history, probably that of Eastern Europe. But there were very few fellowships for graduate study in 1920, and I had had too good a time at Princeton to be in the top tenth of my class. I had accepted my father's dictum that no one can be a good student while working his way through school. Father's financial burdens were still heavy; Julie was at The Johns Hopkins Medical School, and Agnes would soon be ready for college. There was an alternative at hand. I might find a short-term teaching job, save a little money, and then go to graduate school. The interest from that legacy I had received because my names were John Albert should then round out expenses.

A man interviewed me about a position at a mission college in India, but apparently I was not impressive because I never heard any more about it. There was better luck for a job at the Syrian Protestant College, soon to be renamed the American University of Beirut. I knew very little about Lebanon, which had been mandated to the French after the First World War—the books still listed it as being in the Turkish Empire. But there were four students at Princeton whose parents were in Beirut. When Bayard Dodge, later president of the university, interviewed me, my obvious rawness must have been counterbalanced by the recommendation of these fellow students. So I understood that I should begin the teaching of history in the autumn of 1920, just after my twenty-first birthday.

There was some evangelical spirit to my enlistment, even though this college was not a missionary institution. The war was just over, and some of us thought that we might spread the good tidings of American democracy in countries that should be responsive to that message. Surely the good example of education and medical work would be persuasive. It would be a long time before I could see the wisdom of helping other people to find themselves, instead of trying to make them imitation Americans. In the 1920s Americans were still popular abroad. Peoples struggling to become free thought that we would help them. One of my fellow teachers was held up by a gunman in the Lebanon mountains. When the would-be robber learned that he was an American, not a hated Frenchman or an Englishman, there were apologies and an exchange of compliments instead of a robbery.

Early in August 1920, seven young teachers-to-be sailed from New York on the Fabre Line boat, the *Patria*. Throughout the long trip to Naples the old ship maintained a stubborn list to port, which we had to allow for in our games of shuffleboard. We were in second class, which was noisy with Italians returning to their homeland and redolent of Latin cooking. We invaded first class at bouillon time in the morning and at tea time in the afternoon. We found some attractive American girls there. Stops in the Azores, Marseilles, and Palermo gave us distinctly new experiences. The Naples dock was a riot of Italians screaming welcome to their returning relatives, thievish porters, nauseating beggars, and corrupt officials in the custom house. By this time we had assumed a false air of sophisticated assurance, and had even acquired walking sticks, and we fought our way through.

The New York office had bungled our travel plans; we had only four days in Italy instead of three weeks and had to confine our sightseeing to the environs of Naples. Capri, Sorrento, and Amalfi were delightful, and Vesuvius a hot struggle. We rode around Naples in horse-drawn carriages, exercising our limited Italian by pointing to something and asking the driver, *"Cocchiere, che cosa?"* We rarely understood his answer, but it did not matter. We were playing at being young lords on the Grand Tour. Perhaps one passerby was more accurate in describing us as *eccentrici Americani*. An overnight trip by train took us across the insole of Italy. No one had told us that we had to change trains in the middle of the night, but we made it, scrambling across the tracks with all our luggage.

A crowded little Italian steamer took us from Brindisi to Kalamata in Greece, Canea and Candia in Crete, Alexandria and Port Said in Egypt, Jaffa and Haifa in Palestine, and finally Beirut. We had become fat and indolent, with five servings of food a day, and in between stuffing ourselves with Greek grapes, which were piled in open crates on the deck, or with Jaffa melons. At the Beirut dock we were met by the faculty members who were to be our hosts until college opened. That first afternoon one of them took three of us up to his summer home in the mountains. At that time there was practically no motor transportation in the country. We took the little coastal railroad a few miles to a station north of Beirut and then went the rest of the way on foot. As the crow flies our walk may have been about eight miles. But we were fat pigeons, scrambling up zigzag paths over chalky cliffs under a blazing sun. It was a good introduction. We started off with a real respect for the hardiness and the seriousness of our senior professors.

While our party was on the high seas steaming toward Beirut, there was still fighting between the Arabs and the French in the Lebanon mountains. Communications between Beirut and New York were inadequate, and I arrived in Beirut to find that I was to spend three years teaching English instead of history. Although I was the youngest of the party of twenty new teachers, it was somehow understood that I was mature, so that I was put into college English instead of going into the preparatory school. Some of my students were older than I. I had had no courses in English since freshman year. I had no understanding of the problems of teaching English as a foreign language, other than to explain and explain again in different words. If I still retained any Brooklyn accent, it disappeared as I tried to enunciate with exactness. The position of short-term teacher was a delight. Although the hours of teaching were moderately heavy and the load of papers to correct a real burden, the students were bright and eager to learn. I was eager to teach. They were warm-hearted, hospitable, and generous to their own disadvantage. Thus began my love affair with the Arabs, which has lasted all my life.

The Beirut American community was very friendly. They had just come out from under the Turkish yoke, which had been oppressive during the war, and we newcomers were solemnly warned to behave ourselves as if we were monks under a vow of austerity. No young man was to be seen with a young woman at any time, unless there was adequate chaperoning. We should not even walk a girl home from Sunday morning service. The war had so freed social conventions in the United States that such restrictions seemed stodgy and prudish and we often ignored them. But Beirut was a small restricted community, set in a country where women were not yet free, and the forked tongue of gossip was always flashing. Scandal could be made out of a smile and a wave of the hand. Without any improper behavior we went on and had a good time, encouraged by some of the younger members of the faculty.

Beirut was then a lovely little city, wearing a ruff of green pines around her neck, with her head of red-tiled roofs thrust toward the bluest waters of the Mediterranean. Immediately inland were the majestic mountains. Mount Sunnin was usually snow-capped, which softened its rugged austerity. Although we might complain of the damp chill in winter and the summer humidity, for most of the year the climate was delightful. Week-end excursions to Dog River, Byblos, Sidon, or Tyre were easy, and the Christmas or Easter holidays could be spent on trips to Jerusalem, Damascus, Palmyra, or Aleppo, where my imagination began to people the ancient monuments with Phoenicians or Hebrews or Crusaders. Summer months might be spent on the longer trip to Europe. Our annual salaries consisted of room, board, and $600, so that my 1921 summer in Europe had to be offset in 1922 by an inexpensive stay in Lebanon. Faculty families were always hospitable, and hikes in the mountains provided a stiff but welcome distraction. But I found that it was impossible to save any money on that salary.

Unfortunately I learned very little Arabic. The American community was almost self-sufficient. We picked up only the phrases for asking directions or making purchases. The Arabs always met us more than halfway, and fluid sign language bridged the gap. We never walked past a farm without a sincere invitation to come in and help ourselves to grapes or figs. If one knew the polite phrases of greeting and thanks, that seemed to be enough.

If my field of specialty had tentatively been Eastern Europe, it now changed to the ancient Near East. We visited many old sites: Byblos, while the tombs of the princes were being excavated; Palmyra, as the first civilian party since the war; and Carchemish, before that mound was returned to Turkey. In September of 1922 Daniel Bliss, a fellow teacher, and I made a students' trip through Egypt, traveling third class—or fourth, if there was one. My mind turned definitely to that fascinating ancient culture. On another occasion several of us traveled as deck passengers on a small Italian steamer—no cabin or food— for seventeen days, stopping at such places as Tripoli, Mersin, Rhodes, Antalya, Samos, Izmir, Istanbul, Athens, and Venice. We were young and resilient.

One spring day Walter L. Wright, Jr., known as "Livy," and I decided to travel from Beirut to the ancient port of Byblos as the Phoenicians had. At the Beirut harbor we negotiated for passage on a twenty-foot sailboat carrying cargo. The French authorities at the port had some difficulty deciding what to do about two foreigners who wanted to go outside their jurisdiction for a few hours. They finally wrote in our passports a visa for a *promenade sur la mer*. The boat tacked slowly back and forth against a north wind. The twenty-five-mile run took all day. It was pitch dark on a moonless night when we hove to off Byblos. The old helmsman steered in by sighting on the shape of the Lebanon mountains against the starry sky. He hit the narrow rocky mouth of the little harbor exactly. We ran in with oars that dripped phosphorescent light, and beached the boat on the sandy shore. The two of us spent the night sleeping on the sands, just as the Egyptian envoy Wen-Amon may have done three thousand years earlier when he came to Lebanon for cedar.

In my second year Harold H. Nelson returned to his teaching post at the college after a year's furlough in the States. He had taken his Ph.D. at Chicago under Breasted in the field of Egyptology. Nelson generously offered to give us young teachers an evening course in ancient history. Whether the chief attraction was his good teaching, the inclusion of young ladies in the class, or the delicious cake Mrs. Nelson regularly provided, I nevertheless took the work seriously enough to offer myself in candidacy for a master's degree in ancient history. Professor Stuart Crawford, a veteran worker among the Arabs, gave us a course on the religion of the Semites. Nelson guided my first steps in hieroglyphs and his friendship and enthusiasm gave me that final push into the field of Egyptology.

My M.A. was not a degree of high distinction. The American University of Beirut was trying to find its academic level, between the obligation to be a training school in language and technique and the desire to be a research institution. The medical school had high standards, but the arts and sciences curriculum was chiefly an extension of the basic-tool courses given in the preparatory school. Intellectual curiosity was present, but the university was located in an area where there was a high premium on mere memory, and there were too many untrained teachers, like myself. Since the Second World War the university has focused on the social and ecological problems of the Near East and has high performance in many fields. But when I took my master's degree in 1923 it was not clear about graduate study and I had too easy a time. Advanced degrees were so new that they were not ready for them. As the slow academic procession started toward the commencement exercises, a faculty wife walked along with us, doing the last stitching on the hood hanging down a candidate's back.

So now it was to be Egyptology. I wrote home in great enthusiasm about my choice. Father consulted the professor of Hebrew and Old Testament at Union Theological Seminary, who gave the traditional advice: one really had to go to Germany for a doctor's degree, and there were no openings for Egyptologists in the United States. Each warning had its justification. America had almost no university positions in the field, and only the University of Chicago offered a graduate program of any strength. Yet I clung stubbornly to my choice. Then in the spring of 1923 Breasted made a visit to Beirut, and Nelson introduced me to him. With Breasted it was no disqualification that I was starry-eyed. He himself was an enthusiast and could respond to such eagerness. He was just beginning to build up the Oriental Institute at the University of Chicago and was looking for young Americans. On Nelson's recommendation I was offered a magnificent fellowship of $800 a year. I was in.

At Beirut I was still young and still able to make firm friendships. As at Princeton, I found three with whom I could share my life— Dan Bliss, Livy Wright, and my roommate, George A. Hutchinson, who went on after Beirut to help people find and hold jobs in New York State. Then there were the girls. There were five American misses in Beirut, and the corresponding number of interested males was more than twenty. Social life in that community was very brisk for young ladies. A laboratory technician at the University Hospital, Mary Rouse, captured my admiration and then my heart. She still has them.

Beirut in the early 1920s retained a nineteenth-century innocence. In Ras Beirut, where the university was, the dusty lanes were hedged with cactus. Mail took three weeks to come from the United States. Our own community was small. All of the accessible Americans in Lebanon and Syria could sit down together for Thanksgiving dinner. It was leisurely. We might ride the trams or even indulge in a horse-drawn carriage, but usually we walked everywhere, swinging our canes and swaggering along under our pith helmets. We played soccer against French army teams or baseball against sailors when the United States ships were in the harbor.

The French were having disciplinary problems in establishing their mandate over the Arabs, but we were dreamily remote from politics, within a university compound insulated against the town. People could be relaxed and friendly. The sun might be fierce and the lanes might be dusty, but the slate roofs were very red, the trees were very green, the sea was very blue, and we were very young.

Today Beirut is a city of incredible bustle and intensity. Cactus lanes have been replaced by high-rise apartment houses. Hotels have cut off access to the old swimming place near Pigeon Rocks. Bathing cabanas crowd the once deserted sands where we rode horseback. Motorcars charge around a corner in a steady stream of traffic. The big world has claimed Beirut, which can dream no more.

FIVE

STUDIES
AT CHICAGO

THE first president of the University of Chicago, William Rainey Harper, had been a very successful teacher of Hebrew and Old Testament. He conceived of a department in which Biblical studies might have the benefit of work in the surrounding fields of ancient history, Assyriology, Egyptology, and Arabic. In 1923 this department was called Semitic Languages and Literatures as it faced in toward Arts and Sciences, or Old Testament as it faced out toward the Divinity School. The emphasis was philological.

Breasted in 1895 was the first teacher to offer regular courses in Egyptology in any American university. He was a man of extraordinary vision and enthusiasm. In 1919 he captured the interest of John D. Rockefeller, Jr., which enabled him to organize the Oriental Institute as a research partner of the department. When I came to Chicago in 1923 the institute personnel consisted of four research scholars and two technicians. Its growth was to be very rapid in the expansive years of the middle 1920s.

The faculty outnumbered the graduate students. However, in Egyptology there had been an explosion up to three students, two in their second year and myself as a beginner. Since Breasted had had, I believe, only five Ph.D.'s in his previous twenty-eight years of teaching, we three, all at the same time, were exceptional. I was rushed through my beginning courses, using Adolf Erman's little *Aegyptische Grammatik*, so that ancient Egyptian came out with a German accent. Fortunately the study with Nelson had given me a head start. After six months I was tossed in with the second-year students, Edith Ware and William Sassaman. We were reading Papyrus Harris, that great scroll which gave the testamentary enactments of Ramses III on behalf of the temples. It was written in hieratic, the cursive form of hieroglyph, which is closer to the original than demotic, the later form of writing. There was only one copy of the text in Chicago, the 1876 publication by the British Museum, and I sat on the opposite side of the table, transcribed the hieratic upside down, and learned to read it so. That was not a bad introduction to the principle that Egyptian must be read as you see it in its original setting and not as.it is printed in modern books.

Sassaman had to earn his living by driving a taxicab through the entire weekend. He was often both unprepared and very sleepy at the Monday class. Mrs. Ware and I protected him on that day, both by showing a specious eagerness to translate and by asking distracting questions on subjects that interested Breasted. An inquiry about the relative merits of the French approach to Egyptology as contrasted with the German method would be good for a fifteen-minute lecture. After my own forty years of teaching, I cannot believe that we fooled him. He was willing to go along with our game because he knew the circumstances. Despite his busy administrative career he always gave special time and attention to students.

I had three years of the Egyptian language with Breasted and George Allen; a one-year history course with Breasted and D. D. Luckenbill; four quarters of Hebrew with Ira Price and

Godfrey Driver, a visiting Englishman; and four quarters of classical Arabic and three of Islamic history with Martin Sprengling. Nothing was offered in archaeology, art, or religion, and the language study did not go into demotic. By using four quarters a year and writing my dissertation in the third year, I completed the Ph.D. within three years. Today we would not sanction so spotty a curriculum or accept a dissertation guided by a single man. In those days the student program was played by ear rather than by regulation. Further, Breasted was anxious to get me off to the expedition in Egypt as soon as possible.

He was a truly great teacher. Not only was he fully skilled in the Egyptian language and a historian of great discernment, but all his classes had an inspirational excitement. For him grammar and syntax were not merely structure: they offered insights into the psychology of men living thousands of years ago. Verb forms were inventions of the human mind to give greater freedom and precision of expression. This he stated so persuasively that we shared his enthusiasm. Similarly, in his history course, he went right down the middle of the story, brushing aside complexities and uncertainties in order to give us the sweep of mortal triumph and tragedy. If his disciples now work a pedestrian way through the material and emerge with a cautiously balanced conclusion, they can remember the days when the story was made straightforward and exciting.

In those days a student had an awe of the giants who constituted the faculty. If a professor was generous enough to offer advice, the student accepted it with humble gratitude. However, that might depend upon other factors. Twice I was stopped in the corridor of Haskell Oriental Museum for such wisdom. Once the professor of Arabic examined me and made a sweeping vertical gesture. "Wilson, you have a hatchet face"—then a sharp horizontal gesture—"you ought to wear a bow tie." Then there was the professor of Hebrew who said, "Mr. Wilson, if you are determined to go on with this career, you must marry a woman with money." Then he proceeded along the corridor, his shoulders shaking with silent mirth. A small strain of skepticism told me that the thunder from Mount Olympus might sometimes be nothing but thunder.

Off-campus associations were pleasant. My Princeton classmate, Dick Hartshorne, was studying geography at the university. He introduced me to the members of Gamma Alpha, a fraternity for graduate students in the sciences. One day a delegation of them waited on me and asked whether I thought that my work "was scientific." I responded rather fiercely that Egyptologists proceeded carefully with checks and controls, so that of course we moved with scientific method. Perhaps I should not have risen to the bait. Three-quarters of my time was spent on ancient languages and the remainder on history. But "scientific" was an admired word in those days. At any rate, I became a member of Gamma Alpha and learned about physics and geology and physiology from a group of dedicated students. It was a needed antidote to the narrowness of my own curriculum.

The scholarship of $800 was ample for tuition, board and room, and recreation over an eleven-month year. If I exceeded it a little, that was because I made forays eastward to see my family in Connecticut or to pay court to the young lady I had met in Beirut. In the autumn of 1925, when Breasted and Allen were both away in the Near East, I was appointed to the staff of the university as secretary of Haskell Oriental Museum. The visible symbols of my new status were a roll-top desk, the files of the museum, and the cabinet holding all the keys. Perhaps a small hum of importance could have been heard as I assumed my new position.

However, keys express responsibility as well as authority. One morning I discovered that a few scarabs were missing from one of the museum cases. Nobody had worked on that case for some time, and no one could recall when it had last been examined. The university police were summoned. They brought in a detective from the city police, a stocky individual in a derby hat and huge shoes.

He rocked back and forth on his feet and considered the problem. "How do you get into that case?"

"There is a key for it," I answered.

"Only one key?"

"Two keys, but they are always fastened together."

"Where are they?"

"Here they are. They were hanging in their right place in the key cabinet this morning."

"Can anybody get into the key cabinet?"

"No, it's always locked."

"Who has the key to the key cabinet?"

"I do."

"Could anybody else get into that key cabinet?"

"Not unless they got the key from me."

He rocked back and forth silently, while I took in the full implications of this line of questioning. Apparently it was an inside job.

Just then Professor Luckenbill came out of his office. Seeing the unusual number of five persons in the south museum hall, he joined us to find out what the excitement might be. When the problem was explained to him, he said, "Oh, these old cases!" He took out a penknife, went around to the back of the case, removed the four screws that held the hinges, lifted the cover of the case from the rear, and put his hand inside. The detective still looked dubious, but he wrote his report and went away. Luckenbill had rescued the career of a young man in Egyptology.

Breasted had secured some photographs of new inscriptions— or, rather, photographs of new versions of old inscriptions— brought to light by clearances of temples at Luxor and Abydos. He put these at my disposition for a dissertation, "The Texts of the Battle of Kadesh." Shortly after 1300 B.C., Ramses II had fought the Hittites and their allies at a place called Kadesh in northern Syria. At best the pharaoh had staved off defeat, but he plastered the walls of his temples in Egypt with claims of a great victory. My translation and commentary on these texts were not bad for a novice, but today higher standards of collation and comprehension are demanded from the students. The plan had been to continue this work when I went out into the field, by collating all texts on the spot and publishing a definitive edition. However, an able French scholar issued a thoroughgoing compilation of the same material two years later, quite overshadowing my efforts. The disappointment at being anticipated was softened by a suspicion that I was not yet quite ready.

Sprengling knew that he would be out of the country at the time of my final oral examination in late May 1926. He told me not to worry about any testing of my ability in classical Arabic as he had been satisfied with my performance in class. So I dropped that field out of my consideration and I boned up assiduously on other subjects. The examination itself dragged on for three hours. For well over two hours Breasted took me over the hurdles in hieroglyphic, hieratic, and history. The rest of the department sat back in boredom. Since Breasted's current interests were pretty well known, that long grind went off satisfactorily. Then he turned me over to the other examiners. There were a few desultory questions, and my answers were less precise because I was rather weary by that time. Then Breasted announced that, since the examiner in Arabic was not present, he himself would set some questions. The shock of that unexpected attack emptied my brain. Not only could I not translate the Arabic, I could not even pronounce it. It was a sorry performance.

At long last I was excused and went outside into the museum to wait for the examining committee to make its decision. I was in despair. How could they pass me after such a collapse? The wait seemed interminable. Finally the secretary for the department, George Allen, came out to summon me. In his characteristically cautious way he told me first that they had been disappointed. Then he went on to elaborate: instead of passing me *summa cum laude*, they had been forced to pass me only *magna cum laude*.

On the basis of the examination alone a mere pass would have been gratifying.

In those days students did not marry until they had finished their studies and were assured of a salaried position. Breasted told me to report in October to the Oriental Institute's Epigraphic Survey in Egypt. I hurried east, and there was a double wedding in Worcester, Massachusetts, in June 1926. Dan Bliss, who had just finished his studies at Union Theological Seminary, married Winifred Rouse, and I married her sister Mary. The four of us had met in Beirut. Winnie had been the head of the American Community School, and Mary, as I have mentioned, had worked in the hospital. Is it any wonder that the four of us have a special affection for that part of the world?

When Mary and I applied to the city clerk of Worcester for a marriage license he asked my profession. I answered proudly, "Egyptologist." He asked me how to spell it. When he asked Mary's profession she said, "Bacteriologist." He asked how to spell that. Then he said dryly, "Well, you two won't have much competition."

SIX

᭜᭜᭜᭜᭜᭜᭜᭜᭜᭜

WESTERN THEBES

Travel in the 1920s was a leisurely delight. The boat trip between New York and Alexandria took about three weeks in mild summer weather. Since the family exchequer was already low, Mary and I spent only a few days in Cairo and then took the overnight train to Luxor, sitting up in second class. We arrived laden with smoke, dust, and lassitude. Then came a rowboat crossing of the Nile to the west bank and a two-mile drive in a rickety station wagon to old Chicago House, behind the Colossi of Memnon. This was to be our home for the next five years.

Although I had been guilty of prideful exaggeration when I told the members of Gamma Alpha that Egyptology was scientific because it operated within a system of checks and controls, this was an anticipation of what was to come. Between the First World War and the Depression of the 1930s there was an extraordinarily productive decade of field work. The popular symbol of this excitement was the discovery of the tomb of Tut-ankh-Amon in 1922 by Howard Carter, the British archaeologist. The scientific value of those materials lay in their wealth of accumulation rather than in any distinctively new objects or facts. But the discovery ignited an explosion of interest in ancient Egypt among the general public, which resulted in material support for field work. Carter's single-mindedness in demanding that he be allowed to clear the tomb in his own way and at his own pace served notice that Egyptology was a responsible business and not a treasure hunt. This new kindling of interest was like that around 1800, when Napoleon led an expedition to Egypt. Modern communications made the 1922 discovery a matter of daily excitement.

There were many signs of serious purpose in the middle 1920s. On behalf of the Harvard-Boston Expedition at Gizah, George A. Reisner's assistants spent ten uncomfortable months cramped down at the bottom of a pit, sorting out the scattered remnants of the funerary furniture of a Fourth Dynasty queen. Their important results came out of painstaking method, that same system of checks and controls. At Deir el-Bahri in western Thebes, Herbert E. Winlock was showing that logical procedure and constant supervision of the work would produce important findings in an area supposed to be exhausted. Not all of the excavation showed that discipline. The French expedition at Deir el-Medineh had highly valuable results, but a benign paternalism toward the workers let a disproportionate amount of the objects leak into the local antiquities market. Accurate recording of every step in digging must combine with constant supervision of the work to produce a trustworthy product. At Karnak the repair work on the temples was not accompanied by a thorough recording or photography or by an adequate inquiry into Egyptian history, so that it is now difficult to reconstruct just what was found at each point.

New publications were paving the dusty road into Egyptology and providing a firmer surface for progress. In 1919, Heinrich Schaefer issued a book in which Egyptian art was treated in its own terms rather than in Western conceptions. The first volume of *The Cambridge Ancient History* was issued in 1923. The great Berlin dictionary of the ancient Egyptian language began to appear in 1925, giving a translator a tighter control of the language, as well as some assurance that the material had been comprehensively covered. In 1923 Erman published a reliable translation of the literary texts known up to that time, and in 1927 Gardiner's *Egyptian Grammar* was a light for the first footsteps in the Egyptian language and a valued reference book for the more mature scholars. From such works as these the control of materials and methods became firmer.

There was a major setback in 1925–26. Through the agency of Breasted, John D. Rockefeller, Jr., had offered the Egyptian Government $10,000,000 for a new museum and an institute to train Egyptians to administer their own antiquities. We shall never know all of the forces of uncertainty, suspicious nationalism, and international jealousy that led to the withdrawal of this offer in the spring of 1926. However, the years have shown that the collapse of the enterprise was a disaster not only for Egypt but also for Egyptology. In part the slack was taken up by teaching the subject at the University of Cairo, where a group of bright young Egyptians was introduced to scholarship on their own past. Again in retrospect, the brilliant promise of the 1920s for Egyptian scholars was not fulfilled in later years, when the pressure of the governmental system demanded bureaucratic performance instead of scholarly publication. Today there is still eagerness to learn, but this becomes dampened by the necessities of office holding, which discourage imaginative scholarship.

At any rate, when Mary and I went to Luxor in 1926, Egyptology was still in a vigorous period. The atmosphere was charged with faith and promise. My own work was on a new frontier of copying ancient texts.

Epigraphy, the copying of scenes and texts, went back in Egypt more than a century, to Napoleon's expedition. Sometimes an Egyptologist jotted down notes in a copybook, sometimes an artist made accurate drawings of a single scene. It was highly selective. Epigraphy reached new standards when the Egypt Exploration Society set up the Archaeological Survey to make records in the tombs. Norman and Nina Davies, the gifted British artists, were busy copying tombs in western Thebes. Their hands and eyes were specially skilled in capturing line and spirit faithfully. Others who followed similar methods of combining measurement and free hand were less reliable.

When Breasted had made his first trip to Egypt in 1894, he had been appalled at the amount of standing material that had been badly copied or not copied at all. No single temple had been thoroughly studied. Further, excavation had freed tombs and temples from their protecting sand, so that they were deteriorating markedly. He felt that a careful recording of visible evidence was more important than the excavation of further material. That became a cardinal principle for his work in Egypt. He might promote Oriental Institute excavation in other countries, but the chief responsibility in Egypt was to record the monuments incompletely known. On his Nubian expeditions of 1905–1907 he developed a rapid method of copying. After a wall surface had been photographed, a collation of the inscriptions would be made directly on the photographic print. That grew into the Chicago method, applied to the scenes and inscriptions in the temple of Medinet Habu, which had been built in western Thebes by Ramses III about 1180 B.C. This temple had been chosen because it was historically interesting and comparatively well preserved. Copying it completely was the work of the Epigraphic Survey.

Harold Nelson had left the American University of Beirut in 1924 to direct this expedition. After two seasons of work it became clear that a more exhaustive system of checks was needed to give the wealth of detail in the original carving on the walls. Further, that detail demanded larger plates than had originally been planned. Critical to that decision was the naval battle on the north wall of Medinet Habu. The first carving of this scene had seemed too static to the ancient critics. It had therefore been plastered over, and the new carving had made the Egyptian soldiers lean forward more vigorously to the attack. When the plaster fell out, both versions were visible on the wall. Painstaking collation was necessary to straighten out the lines of one version from those of the other. Certainly demonstration of the ancient criticism and correction was an important contribution to our knowledge of art and psychology.

Breasted and Nelson worked out a system using an enlarged photograph as the base for the drawing of a skilled artist. This preliminary drawing was checked and counterchecked by two Egyptologists. The artist and the Egyptologists had to agree before the drawing was final and inked in, with the photograph faded out chemically. The result combined the accurate dimensions of a photograph, the trained eye and hand of an artist, and the knowledge of texts and scenes possessed by Egyptologists. In that setting we Egyptologists were called "epigraphers," with the accent on the "pig," conforming to the accented "tog" in "photographer."

As art the published plates have a certain harshness and impersonality, which may contrast unfavorably with the grace and personal emotion in the drawings and paintings made by Mr. and Mrs. Davies. However, these are faithful renderings of the Medinet Habu carvings, which were cut deep and bold into uncompromising sandstone, whereas the limestone of the Theban tombs offered a surface for softer and more delicate carving. The elaborate system of checks and counterchecks in the Chicago system has meant that the Medinet Habu publications have taken an unconscionable time to appear. The process has seemed too expensive of time and money for other institutions to follow. However, the finished product has an accuracy unsurpassed by other methods. Since the work was planned to give a definitive record of an ancient monument, that fidelity has certainly been justified. Now, after forty years, the Medinet Habu of Ramses III has been published in its entirety, the only large and uniform monument from pharaonic times so honored. It was a proud experience for a youngster to be associated with an expedition of such high standards, an expedition that was not seeking material objects but a historical record.

Probably my pride in the work showed itself in my carriage. A visitor to Chicago House impatiently asked a staff member, "Who is that cocky little fellow Wilson?" Since there were no secrets on the expedition, I of course soon heard of his question. Years later, unaware that I knew his attitude, the man solemnly assured me, "I spotted you as the coming man in the Oriental Institute as soon as I first saw you."

After Breasted and Nelson had established the proper procedure, the work went smoothly. Medinet Habu was a well-preserved temple because its walls had been used for centuries to support Christian buildings and therefore had not been torn down for other purposes. The solidly carved surface rose up for more than thirty feet, or forty-five feet on the first pylon. Artists and epigraphers spent most mornings standing on high ladders, copying or collating. Afternoons were usually spent at the expedition house, the artists inking in what they had penciled at the wall, the epigraphers checking library books for comparable material. The expedition rapidly built up an Egyptological library, which has become one of the best in Egypt, certainly the pleasantest to work in.

A critical factor in the process is the collation sheet. Physically this is a blueprint made from the artist's first drawing. The blueprint is cut into convenient small strips and pasted on sheets of paper, which can be carried to the wall on a clipboard and suspended from a rung of the ladder while the epigrapher does his checking. It holds the observations made about the carved surface, the arguments as to the visible evidence, and notations made in the library. The collation sheet is both the record of work in process and the justification for drawn line or textual emendations.

The epigraphers criticize the artist's drawing for accuracy and for amplification or deletion of line. In theory the artist and the epigraphers must agree before any drawing is accepted as final. In practice the Egyptologists often oppose their professional knowledge to the professional skill of the artist. Since the end product is intended to be accurate rather than aesthetically pleasing, the artist has usually bowed to the dictates of the epigraphers, even though he may grumble at some of the more finicking demands.

On a collation sheet such a cabalistic notation as "cf. Anast. II, 3:1" would refer to a parallel text that helped in understanding a text or a scene. These working materials are vitally important for supplementary volumes that translate and explain the published plates. Experience has shown that these collation sheets must be used right away for such secondary publication. William F. Edgerton and I did get out a translation of the first two Medinet Habu volumes, but later studies which were proposed were laid aside in the pressure of daily work and went by default. The admirable presentation of scenes and texts in the plate volumes has not been completed by the further analysis of those best qualified by experience to work on them.

It was pleasurable and profitable to be teamed with Edgerton. Billy had studied at Cornell and then taken his doctorate under Breasted at Chicago. Although he was a man of warm dedication, his mind was legal and demanded to see firm evidence before accepting any conclusion. The fervor that Breasted had inspired in me needed to be harnessed by this insistence that documentary proof must be produced to justify any impulsive surge forward. Billy and I stood side by side on ladders at the temple and sat in alcoves across from each other in the library. We soon reached a point where we did not need to talk things out at length. We knew each other so well that we seemed to move together by instinct. Later I found that every good pair of epigraphers has this same experience of teamwork.

This was a professional labor, to give scholars a definitive record of a slowly perishing monument. It was not meant to be a popular publication for the art world. Once a party of tourists entered the temple while I was working on my ladder. In a clear, carrying British voice a lady asked, "Guide, what is that man doing up there?" "Oh," said the dragoman in regal scorn, "he is writing a book—but no one will read it!" Those who could read the hieroglyphic texts of Ramses III were very few indeed.

Old Chicago House was a sprawling complex of mud brick. The living quarters were on our own land, and the working quarters—drafting rooms, library, offices, darkroom, storerooms, and servants' quarters—were on government land. Much of the structure was new, and scorpions loved to come out on the damp brick at night. The lacing of timbers inside the mud brick and the wooden roofing became riddled with termites. In 1931 the expedition had to find a more permanent home across the river, to the regret of those who loved the west side.

The old living room lay under a high dome. Legend said that when the house was built the contractor had been too stingy to make a sacrifice to the jinn of that particular piece of land. When the dome had reached a certain height, the walls would not support the weight of a man. A boy was detailed to lay the bricks as they centered in for the final arch. He fell off and was killed. The workmen then deserted the job. The contractor had to kill two sheep at the threshold, to appease the jealous jinn, before the workmen would return to the job. Such stories, whether true or not, were common in that simple setting.

The household was cosmopolitan. The three Egyptologists—Nelson, Edgerton, and I—were American. The three artists came from Germany, Italy, and England. The photographer was Austrian, and the librarian British. There were also the members of the Architectural Survey, which was excavating the Medinet Habu complex, several wives, a child, and various attendants. Not counting a few regular visitors, twenty-two persons from five different countries sat down for three meals a day. At the end of an intensive six-month season they would be heartily tired of one another. This has been a normal experience on every field expedition I have known. It did not break friendships, which remained warm after the season ended and the daily pressure was relieved.

Our provincial home was the center of things archaeological. A dozen temples and hundreds of tombs were close by for visiting on our day off each week. Just to the west of us the French were digging at Deir el-Medineh. The German House was five minutes away to the northwest. Mr. and Mrs. Davies emerged every day from their little house near Sheikh Abd el-Gurneh to copy in the tombs. The Metropolitan House faced Deir el-Bahri, where Winlock and his staff were working. Carter's house was perched on a height near the road leading to the Valley of the Kings, where he was still clearing the tomb of Tut-ankh-Amon. We were too busy for much social activity, but we lived so close together that we saw each other rather often. Winlock's visits were always amusing, as he had a bluff way of bringing stuffy or romantic persons down to earth with a thump. Carter was more formal, although he once called in his pajamas in the hot weather just before the season opened and had to beat a hasty retreat when he found that one of our ladies had already arrived.

The visitors were interesting. Alan Gardiner would stay with us for a few days while he checked Theban texts of his current interest. Adriaan de Buck stopped over to confer with Breasted and Gardiner before he began the long work of copying the Coffin Texts, so called because the texts were found on wooden coffins of the Middle Kingdom. Henri Frankfort, digging at Armant ten miles to the south, would come and share his exuberance with us. Excavators from other countries would stay for a few days because Breasted happened to be currently at Chicago House—Oriental Institute diggers from Megiddo in Palestine or Alishar in Turkey. Mikhail I. Rostovtzev, fresh from his dig on the Euphrates, let us know in very candid terms what he thought of the sumptuousness of this house of Breasted's. Kenneth S. Sandford and W. J. Arkell, two young British prehistorians, launched their Prehistoric Survey from Chicago

House, going out in their light little car to bump along the edges of the desert cliffs.

Then there were the briefer visits for luncheon or tea or business: cocky little Ludwig Borchardt and big friendly Georg Steindorff; Wilhelm Spiegelberg, collecting the graffiti scratched on the Theban hillsides; Pierre Lacau, the imposing director-general of the Antiquities Service in Egypt; F. L. Griffith, just back from excavations in the Sudan; and many others, to our great profit.

Nonscholarly visitors were sometimes a burden but more often a pleasure. There were the imposing Aga Khan, friendly John Masefield, and voluble Sir Robert Mond. A British noble-man, hearing that Mary was going to Germany with me but did not know the language, gave her a German sentence with which to greet her teacher. Translated into English, the sentence ran, "Thou hast a donkey between the ears." There was the woman who introduced herself as the mistress of H. G. Wells, and the American businessman who was going around counting temple doorways in order to check Homer's epithet, "hundred-gated Thebes."

The two most momentous visits were by the Rockefeller family and by Elisabeth, Queen of the Belgians. Breasted es-corted the Rockefellers through the Near East. He carefully did not ask for more money, since Mr. Rockefeller had already been so generous. But John D., Jr., was genuinely interested in what he saw, Breasted was an enthusiastic guide, and the visit came during the prosperous time of early 1929, so that there was an expansion of Oriental Institute activities in Egypt. For one thing, the expedition got the fine new house on the east bank.

Queen Elisabeth was alert to the fascination of antiquity. She wanted to see everything. She was also adventurous. The first pylon at Medinet Habu had proved too high for our ladders. A steel beam was laid on top of the pylon, and a boatswain's chair was suspended from this beam by a pulley. Thus one of us could be hauled up to his work and sit there comfortably, lashed firmly in place forty feet above the ground. Her Majesty expressed the wish to go up in this chair. That caused some anxious moments, as the carvings were as much as three inches deep and she wore moderately high heels. Happily, it turned out to be only an exhilarating experience.

When Queen Elisabeth heard that our infant daughter was at Chicago House, she asked to see the child, as she had a granddaughter of the same age. Sometimes a thirteen-month-old baby is fretful if awakened from a nap. But Peggy turned out to be a little courtier: she accepted a royal handshake and did not clutch at the string of pearls dangling right in front of her. Her Majesty's visit to the temple and the house went off so well that the subsequent award of the Order of Leopold to Harold Nelson seemed amply justified.

In the late 1920s Germany was still the center of good Egyptology. Breasted and Nelson encouraged me to study there during vacation. I spent one summer under Kurt Sethe, in Berlin, and another working at demotic under Spiegelberg in Munich. In a substantive way, these studies did not advance me as much as the specific research at Luxor. But the European experience and the friendly atmosphere of pre-Hitler Germany were a valuable part of my education.

Once a field man always a field man. I have not written about the beauty of our landscape in Egypt, about our recreational activities, or about the pleasure of our field trips. It is enough to remember an intensive research in a rich setting. In the following forty years I have made only occasional forays into the field. Yet, like the Greek mythological figure Antaeus, I feel that I gain new strength every time my feet touch the soil. I may live and work in Chicago, but the vigorous renewal has come from my returns to Egypt.

SEVEN

A TEACHER
AT CHICAGO

Edgerton had gone to teach at the University of Chicago in 1929. But he wanted to return to Egypt for one year to collate demotic graffiti in the temple of Medinet Habu. So I was to take his place at the university for the one year 1931–32, with the rank of "Visiting Assistant Professor," and thereafter return to Luxor. That one year stretched out to thirty-seven years before retirement solved the problem of my place and function. To begin with, it was recognized that graduate teaching of Egyptology leading to the doctor's degree needed more than one teacher. Edgerton soon took over the later phases of the language, Late Egyptian, demotic, and Coptic, while I undertook the older phases, hieroglyphic and hieratic. After we had worked out what a comprehensive program should be, two men were not enough, so that in 1936 Keith Seele was brought back from the Luxor expedition to round out the teaching.

Another reason for remaining in Chicago was a growing family. There were two infant children by the autumn of 1931.

Field archaeologists have often taken their young children out on expeditions, but health uncertainties and the later problem of schooling are difficulties that have never been fully solved.

Could I teach beginning hieroglyphic, beginning Coptic, and a course in Ptolemaic inscriptions, all on the graduate level? I was willing to give it a good trial. There may have been some doubts, because at the end of that first year Breasted recommended that I remain on the faculty, reporting that my teaching had been more successful than had been anticipated. In long retrospect, I can see that I probably fell short on the Coptic and mangled the Ptolemaic. The hieroglyphic, which was the beginning course for the entire program, went off better. Sitting down with stimulating students, I found myself simply their senior partner in the attack on Gardiner's *Egyptian Grammar*. In order to capture that slight seniority I had to work much harder than they. I constructed grammatical patterns to illustrate the language, so that the memory might be aided by the sort of thing that appears as *amo, amas, amat* in Latin. I have never been able to sit back and feel assured that at last I know. It is a matter of trying and trying again. There are some inscriptions that I have offered my classes in Old Egyptian for thirty years, but I keep working at them in the hope that I can make them a little more intelligible. If I gave a course or a lecture in exactly the same way I should begin to bore myself—and the students would share that boredom.

For our field the class in beginning hieroglyphic was large—four students—and I had two in Coptic and three in Ptolemaic. The course in the history of ancient Egypt, given in the summer of 1932, was a different matter. In those days summer school was a tremendous enterprise. Teachers from colleges and secondary schools flocked in eager crowds to the University of Chicago for refresher courses or added knowledge. My room was filled with mature, attentive students. In those days it was unthinkable to conduct a class unless you wore a coat and necktie. At noontime, through Chicago's hottest summers, I stood up there fully clad, literally sweating out a subject matter that I wanted to make lucidly clear. After such a class I would resort to the university swimming pool for a refreshing dip before going to lunch.

In order to get the history clear in my own thinking, I made graphs and charts for my classes. They showed the succession of prehistoric pottery, the chronology of dynasties in the dark periods, or the different aspects of a two-dimensional art. Although the students seemed to grasp this audio-visual teaching readily, it may have had a negative factor, since I came to rely more on my own drawings than on lantern slides. The students were robbed of photographs of landscape, temples, statues, or jewelry because of my passion for drawing my own graphs and charts.

The attempt to convey interest in the subject sometimes drove me to dramatics. I might express my admiration for the administrative genius of Thut-mose III or my scorn for the boastfulness of Ramses II. Years later a student commented on the show I put on. She said that when I asserted my contempt for the alleged "curse of King Tut" the atmosphere in class was as tense as though I had lifted my face, defying the lightning to strike. Well, I was a disciple of a great master of persuasive rhetoric, James Henry Breasted.

Those stimulating summers came to an end with the Depression. State educational systems discouraged teachers from taking enrichment courses in subject matter at a big university and corralled them at home for pedagogical courses. These may have been less expensive, but there was a loss to the teachers, their schools, and to the universities.

My first history lessons must have been naïve and simplistic. Many of the intricate problems did not then appear to be problems. I was able to glide over them. But there was always a nagging question: Why? Why did thus-and-so happen in history? Further, since no one else was teaching archaeology, I put that into my history course. Without my realizing it at first, my history was shifting from political–philological to cultural–archaeological. I was trying to find the socio–economic and the psycho-logical–spiritual backgrounds to what we could already see as political development. Since the question "Why?" can rarely be adequately answered, the attempt to find reason goes on indefinitely. But it does make the offering less factual and more speculative.

A few years later Henri Frankfort returned from field work, and then archaeology was formally presented in our curriculum. I had a chance to listen in on his seminar in comparative stratigraphy—that is, the attempt to correlate the cultural levels as they appeared in the excavations at different points of the ancient Near East. Since several of the Oriental Institute field expeditions were terminated, a bright constellation of archaeologists was in Chicago, preparing publication. Many of the participants in Frankfort's seminar were specialists in their separate fields. An eavesdropper sitting on the sidelines could see that one must first formulate the important questions before one could look for satisfactory answers.

For that attempt to frame the right questions the anthropologist Robert Redfield was very helpful. He let some of us attend his seminar on The Folk Society. Redfield set up two theoretical concepts as the contrasting opposites in human society, a "primitive" folk society at one extreme and a "modern" urbanized society at the other. It was not a matter of the modern being highly developed and therefore "good," so that the primitive was "bad." Each theoretical culture was coherent in itself and therefore right for itself. It was good for me to have a purely theoretical framework against which to measure the ancient Egyptians as they proceeded through the centuries. It was high time to abandon the wistful notion that man's historical course has been inevitably upward. It was time to see that a primitive society had its own complexity and its own high morality, whereas a modern urbanized society had retained savagery and superstition. Father could probably have told me that fifteen years earlier, but I had to discover it for myself.

Any teacher, like any parent, has a mixture of pride and envy as his juniors surpass him. We try to teach them to be better, and that should mean better than we are. However, it is difficult to shake off the attitude that we are the masters and they are the disciples. So, with pride and envy, I here record that a half-dozen of my former students have outstripped me in their command of language and history. Egyptology is a small world and highly competitive. There are only two dozen professional Egyptologists in the United States. The best students have to be very good to win the few positions available.

A research project I accepted in the early 1930s never came to completion. Breasted turned over to me photographs and notes from his Nubian copying expeditions of 1905–1907. For some months I worked on them for publication, but then my enthusiasm dampened. After the epigraphic work at Luxor, I could not accept any substitute for personal collation of an inscription on the site. Like Doubting Thomas, I wanted to put my fingers on the evidence and not to rely upon the testimony of others, including photographs—perhaps especially photographs of carved surface that had deteriorated over the centuries. The work was shelved against the possibility that I might someday go to Nubia and collate for myself. Meanwhile I was collecting translations of old and new texts and constantly revising the notes for the course in Egyptian history. Both sets of manuscripts would be tested over the years and ultimately be published.

Breasted had created the Oriental Institute, secured funds for it, and formed its staff. In the new institute building, four workers out of five owed their jobs to him. Now the great Depression lay over the land, and there were no jobs elsewhere. Even in that financial crisis, when the opportunity appeared to start work at Persepolis in Iran, Breasted was able to find the money for this important dig. Only he and the executive secretary, his son Charles, knew what was going on in the dozen or more projects of the institute. Breasted ran the show, with courteous bows to the professors and to the university administration. The institute could not have been built up so fast and so effectively in any other way. In those days there were no audible complaints from the workers under him. Possibly there were murmurs in the president's office and the board of trustees, where Breasted's financial freedom was not so much admired. Later the administration told me that I might not solicit money in competition with the university, as they claimed Breasted had done.

The rapid growth of the institute was not wholly to its good. Many of the new persons appointed were inexperienced, and some of them were temperamental. With so many enterprises, the new findings were coming in too fast for scholarship to comprehend them. Breasted knew this, but with remarkable prescience he said, some time before 1930, that the Near East might offer about ten years of productive field work before local nationalism and world finances would slow the work down. He overestimated the time but not the urgency of doing what was possible while conditions were nearly ideal out in the field.

In 1935 there were nine active field expeditions of the Oriental Institute, five in Egypt and one each in Palestine, Syria, Iraq, and Iran. Four projects had finished field work and were busy at publication. The *Handbook* for that year listed sixty-two persons on the field expeditions and fifty-seven on the staff at home. The total budget was more than $600,000 for 1935–36, a very large amount for that time.

It was in 1935 that I was promoted to associate professor of Egyptology, with tenure on the faculty, appointed secretary of the department, and made scientific secretary of the institute. I understood that the two secretarial jobs were housekeeping chores. A junior member of the staff was being assigned to certain higher clerical chores. These included answering letters from persons volunteering to work for the institute or from institutions seeking collaboration with the institute; responding to the offer of manuscripts to be published at institute cost; and talking with people who had genuine or forged antiquities for sale. One of my assignments was to hear and criticize a long poem by Vachel Lindsay about Cleopatra in Hades. The poet assured me that he knew ancient Egypt, because on his poetry-reading trips he used to spend an hour reading the Book of the Dead before going to sleep. That must have been in translation. He read his poem in a private home, before a worshiping group of old ladies. Lindsay threw back his leonine head and rolled out the sonorous passages. The only jarring element was the young scholar taking notes. When Lindsay finished there was enthusiastic applause. Then I trotted out my miserable little corrections. Anubis was a jackal, not a dog; the earth god was Geb, not Seb; and so on. The group showed little patience with such pedantry, and I left the party as soon as I could politely do so.

I may have been naïve, but I did not believe that the position of scientific secretary was the designation of the heir-apparent for the Oriental Institute. I was only thirty-five. Surely Breasted would go on as director indefinitely and would ultimately be succeeded by one of those eminent scholars who were my respected seniors. Meanwhile it was exciting to learn something about the inside of a university and about the outside of a big research enterprise. Nobody could have foreseen what the end of that year 1935 would do to the institute.

One of the perquisites of being scientific secretary was to inspect field activities, and Mary and I set out on a trip that autumn. A lazy ocean crossing brought us to the Nineteenth International Congress of Orientalists in Rome toward the end of September. That was an experience of the interplay of scholarship and international politics. Hitler's Germany was threatening the scholars of Central Europe. A high official of the Italian Government, in his speech welcoming the congress, justified the forthcoming Italian invasion of Ethiopia. Just after the congress we had the shattering experience of standing in the Piazza Venezia and hearing Mussolini give the summons to the Ethiopian war in an emotional speech from the balcony. In many respects I am a stodgy conservative; change seems to me subversive. But that afternoon Mussolini summoned from me some of my father's liberalism. I realized that the superficial order that we observed in that police state came at the cost of personal freedom.

In Egypt it was a delight to be back again on Theban soil. It was a pleasure to see Breasted, at the age of seventy, charging up a steep slope in the Wadi Hammamat to see an inscription he previously had known only from publication. Then there was the love feast at the Continental Hotel in Cairo. For more than thirty years there had been a coolness between Breasted of Chicago and Reisner of Harvard. One can only guess at the roots of their rivalry, but the division had been widened when Reisner had criticized Breasted's part in the Rockefeller offer of a grant for a new museum in Cairo ten years earlier. Also present were Ludwig Borchardt, head of German work in Egypt until the advent of Hitler, and Hermann Junker, head of German work in Egypt under Hitler. So there was a reconciliation party, at which Reisner sat down with Breasted and Borchardt sat down with Junker. Thus was fulfilled the prophecy of Isaiah, although witnesses may differ as to who were the wolves and the leopards and who were the lambs and the kids.

After this party Breasted and his wife started back to the United States by ship, while Mary and I escorted his daughter Astrid through the institute expeditions in Asia.

My specialties were language and history. I was never a dirt archaeologist. At the end of the 1927 season at Luxor, I had gone to Megiddo in Palestine, to spend a few weeks learning about excavation. When Mary and I had arrived, we found that there was not a Western man left at the mound. Malaria had ravaged the staff. Fortunately the work had been well organized, and the mound was marked with a grid of squares for precise location. For two weeks I kept the workmen digging away at the same level. I supervised the moving of earth and listened solemnly to the report of the foreman, of which I understood only about half. At the end of a day I labeled the baskets of finds by square and level and took them into the house for the woman registrar to catalogue. By the time the staff had been reorganized the new director was too busy learning his mound to bother about teaching me. So I ran a dig briefly without knowing the principles and detailed techniques of excavation. Now, on this 1935 trip, the work was better organized, and it was possible to learn more about purposes and procedures.

The great change in the archaeology of western Asia, during the 1920s and 1930s had been the recognition of prehistory and earliest history. Such terms as Early Bronze II or Jemdet Nasr designated ages where inscriptional evidence might be lacking and where the chronology depended upon pottery sequences and interrelations with other cultures. Archaeology was moving away from the philologist as the key figure toward the pottery expert or the prehistorian, because there were often no inscriptions for the philologist to deal with. That was the case in Iraq and in that area of north Syria which was later ceded to Turkey. It was also the case at Megiddo, but the tangled evidence there was too confusing for real clarity. The institute's specialists at the complex of mounds northeast of Baghdad and at the mounds near Antioch were straightening out evidence on a good pioneer basis. By listening and looking one could learn a lot. The sense of discovery was strong in the field. People wanted to talk about their new finds.

The problem was to organize and arrange into a series the pottery and cylinder seals and walls and doors appearing in stratified mounds, where the older regularly lay under the later. Thus periods of time running out of the prehistoric into the historic might be identified. This practice was still new at the time. What Frankfort and his staff were doing in the Diyala Valley of Iraq and what Calvin McEwan and Robert Braidwood were doing in the Amuq plain of Syria became normative for later work. To repeat the same kind of work a generation later would enlarge the repertoire of forms and places, without adding anything distinctively new. The study of prehistory still uses stratigraphy wherever possible and sets up a pottery corpus, if there is pottery, but it has shifted its goals. It has ceased to be classical, clinging to the edge of the period of written history, and has become ecological. It still asks where men lived and worked and worshiped, but it has focused on the questions of how they lived and what they had to eat. The frontier has pushed out into new territory with new problems.

At the camp in Syria a British archaeologist, Max Mallowan, and his wife came through on the way to their dig in Iraq. The men had a vigorous discussion about walls, levels, and pottery. Mrs. Mallowan sat patiently through it all. She seemed to have little gossip to share with the American women. Before they departed they signed the guest book. Only then did we discover that she was the great writer of mystery stories, Agatha Christie.

Late in November 1935, Astrid Breasted, Mary, and I were on a steamer docked in the harbor of Basra. We were to go to Bushire in Iran and then drive up to Shiraz and visit the institute dig at Persepolis. We had finished a good curry luncheon and were watching the people down on the dock. They were from Baluchistan, had made a pilgrimage to Kerbela, and now were waiting to board the steamer for the return home. Many of them were taking back a souvenir from their journey, a lantern made out of a shiny gasoline tin. They were as fascinated by us as we were fascinated by them. At this point we received a message that landslides had closed the road between Bushire and Shiraz. Our trip to Persepolis had to be canceled. We hurried from the boat to the Basra railroad station, where the overnight train to Baghdad was just ready to leave. We had exhausted our Iraqi money. Tickets, berths, and meals on the train would come to a pretty dinar. I rushed up to the porter of the sleeping car, who was standing on the platform checking the passengers in, and asked excitedly, "Where can I get some money changed?"

He looked at me calmly. "How much money do you want?"

I made a rapid mental calculation. "I'd like to change one hundred dollars in American Express checks into dinars."

The porter produced a fat wallet. "I will give you the money."

Of course he knew that three Americans could not drop out of sight in Iraq and that he would not lose by his generosity.

So we were sitting in a Baghdad hotel, trying to keep warm on a cold, rainy day. We could not return to the institute expedition at Tell Asmar because the road had become a thick blubber of mud. A cablegram from the United States was handed to us: Dr. Breasted had been taken seriously ill; we should cut our trip short and return immediately.

We made the fastest trip between Baghdad and Chicago that archaeology had heard of at the time—ten days. An Imperial Airways plane took us from Baghdad to Alexandria, where the British fleet had congregated to watch the Italian adventure in Ethiopia. A seaplane took us to Brindisi in Italy. Then there was a train to France. The fast liner *Europa* carried us across the Atlantic. We were already too late. When our plane had touched down in Gaza for refueling, another cablegram had reached us. Dr. Breasted had died in New York on the second of December. We returned to a world overcast with grief and uncertainty.

EIGHT

DIRECTOR OF THE ORIENTAL INSTITUTE

THE British *Journal of Egyptian Archaeology* stated in 1935: "The death of Professor James Henry Breasted . . . has deprived the world not only of one of the greatest figures in the history of Egyptology, but also of the foremost living American Orientalist, a scholar whose activities and interests embraced the whole of the ancient Near East, and an administrator and publicist of unsurpassed energy." He served Egyptology "as organizer and Director of the Oriental Institute of the University of Chicago, into the multifarious enterprises of which, from its creation in 1919, he threw an immense amount of energy, making it, with funds supplied by Mr. John D. Rockefeller, jun., by far the greatest centre of archaeological research which has hitherto existed. . . . His charming and stimulating personality was a delight to all who knew him; in this connexion we may quote from a letter to *The Times* by Dr. Gardiner, his closest friend in this country: 'Breasted was not a man to be easily diverted from his labours, but when at last so diverted he could play like a child and was a companion of extraordinary charm. He enjoyed talking and had many a good story at his disposal. An unbounded enthusiasm, which a touch of *naïveté* rendered doubly infectious, gave a singular attraction to his conversation, and his handsome features and athletic figure added greatly to the pleasure afforded by his society.' "

So strong were Breasted's persuasive charm and his optimism that he probably could have ridden out any severe crisis. However, his sudden death spared him the knowledge of the troubles that were to come. The trustees of the University of Chicago were trying to finance the institution through the continuing years of the Depression. As a measure of economy they were retiring eminent scholars who were seventy years old, hiring younger men, and thus replacing high salaries by low. If the Grand Old Man of football, Amos Alonzo Stagg, had to retire, would Breasted have been spared?

Further, Breasted did not live to read a letter from Rockefeller that warned him that the Rockefeller boards could not afford to continue their annual support of the Oriental Institute and would have to conclude their interest in archaeology by a terminal grant. As for himself, Rockefeller prized his friendship with Breasted very much, but he also would be forced to withdraw from support of the institute's activities. All these blows were consequences of the Depression. They were only coincidental with the death of the man. Yet the combination of losses made it seem that the institute, soaring up like a comet, might crash like a meteorite.

Not all of this was realized at the beginning of 1936. All of us were in a state of shock from Breasted's death. When I was appointed acting director—the full position came six months later—my chief feeling was a sense of duty to carry on. The mantle of Elijah had been too heavy for Elisha at first. He was indecisive. When the "sons of the prophets" wanted to go seeking the vanished Elijah, his successor Elisha first told them not to go, then let them go, and then, after they had returned from a fruitless search, reminded them that he had opposed their going. A prophet should be made of sterner stuff. Through the winter and spring of 1936 I became aware of the task laid upon me. Fortunately, Charles Breasted generously offered to stay on as assistant director for several months. Without his knowledge of purposes, persons, and procedures, there would have been chaos.

In addition, I came home to a controversy quite unrelated to the problems of maintaining the institute. The chairman of the Department of Oriental Languages and Literatures, Martin Sprengling, had seen a major gap in the curriculum and was planning a program for the teaching of archaeology, including a technique in which several potential instructors were skilled—a course in archaeological photography. Richard McKeon, dean of the Division of the Humanities, objected that this might be appropriate in a technical training school but was no proper subject for the humanities. A result of the dispute was that Sprengling resigned his chairmanship, and I found myself appointed chairman of the department. Seven professors were senior to me in years, experience, and demonstrated scholarship. However, the department and the institute have always been intertwined. Any major influence in one inevitably affected the other. Reconstruction of the institute would involve some reconstitution of the department. In that process the university administration may have wished to watch one man instead of two.

My father had happened to be staying with the parents of Robert M. Hutchins when it was announced that that young man was to be the next president of the University of Chicago. Father was exuberant. "This is wonderful! Let's shout it from the rooftops! Let's turn out the band!" Mrs. Hutchins said solemnly, "We think that it is not so much a matter for shouting as a matter for prayer." Now I was the one standing in the need of prayer.

Before 1936 the Oriental Institute had had something in the range of $2,000,000 in endowment. The remainder of the annual budgets had been made up by grants from the Rockefeller boards. The Rockefeller Foundation had offered Breasted another million if he could match it from other sources. He had not lived to make that attempt. So, even in their current financial stringency, the boards decided upon a very generous action. Their General Education Board itself provided the matching million, so that $2,000,000 came as a terminal grant. The grant carried a stipulation that this money was to be for the use of the institute over a period of ten years. Thereafter the trustees might determine its further application. At the time this condition did not loom as important. I was too busy calculating that a budget which annual grants had brought up to more than $600,-000 a year would have to be cut back to that $200,000 which income might provide.

Mr. Rockefeller and the officers of the Rockefeller boards were fully aware of the consequences of such a cutback and treated me with every consideration. David H. Stevens, the Foundation's director for the Humanities, was understanding and sympathetic. On a cool March day we went over the situation, and then he took me for a walk through the Central Park Zoo in New York, talking about the animals, the political situation in Europe, his summer home in Wisconsin—anything except finances.

An obvious solution was to go out and seek other funds to keep up the work. That was not so easy. The Depression lay across the land like a black incubus. The Oriental Institute had been so definitely a Rockefeller project that no other major source of support would be willing to step in to pick up the maintenance. Further, I was asked not to solicit funds in competition with the efforts of the university. This ruled out some of the obvious sources. In one of our first long talks, President Hutchins asked me whether I wanted to make the institute socially popular, so that fashionable Chicago would be attracted to its support. I answered rather flatly that the institute was a research agency and that its dedication to scholarship should not be tinseled over by making it socially appealing. He nodded his understanding. Perhaps I was too snobbish. Fifteen years later Carl Kraeling, then the institute's director, showed that successful "mink-coat parties" in our museum would attract great interest and a modest flow of money without interfering with the research work of the scholars. But the Depression was over by then.

The problem in 1936 was to trim sail and jettison some cargo, while keeping on course and not abandoning ship. We did not have to drop the 1936–37 budget a full two-thirds below the current level. A number of economies could be effected immediately. There could be two staged years to reach the indicated lower level. Some of the economies were in savings in the final three months, and some of them were real sacrifices. Breasted had been able to maintain three excellent budgetary provisions: field archaeologists were on annual salary instead of being picked up for the season only; money was regularly budgeted for those publications which were expected in any one year; and there were ten handsome fellowships for graduate students. The principle of maintaining archaeologists on salary was retained, so that they could prepare publication during the off-season. But the insurance of publication by annual inclusion in the budget had to be surrendered, and money that might have provided for new students had to be diverted to eke out the salaries of current staff members. Both cuts were retreats from good principle, made necessary by the emergency.

The crisis was like that which confronted the legendary Egyptian peasant Goha. While he was rowing across the Nile his boat began to fill with water. He made fervent vows to Allah, but the craft continued to sink. He threw out a big bag of beans, but that did not lighten the boat enough. He threw out his wife, but still they were foundering. Finally he threw out his donkey. In a few moments the boat came to rest on a sandbank. "Oh Allah," Goha cried, "I praise Thy Providence! I praise Thy compassionate and merciful Name! But couldn't You have let me know in the first place that it was the donkey You wanted?" I might have lightened the institute load by throwing myself overboard. There were others in the same boat who insisted that they were not donkeys.

There had to be drastic surgery. In place of nine field expeditions, there were only two, the Epigraphic Survey at Luxor with a reduced staff and a small excavation to test some clearly restricted problem in some other country. Some expeditions were canceled summarily. Others were put on notice that they would have to resolve their major problems in one or two more years. In every case there was an attempt to retain those scholars who were needed to see the work through to publication.

Of the approximately one hundred and twenty staff members at home and abroad, more than forty-five had to receive notice of termination, immediately or in the near future. Detailed letters went to those abroad, explaining the cut. I had long talks with those at home. It was necessary to deal sympathetically with the questions, "All right! But why me?" It was to be expected that scholars with a pride in their work would ask that question. In one case a research man, faced with ten weeks' notice, took his case to the local chapter of the American Association of University Professors. Three distingiushed scholars of the university visited me and told me that human relations and humane provisions for hiring and firing were more important than budget figures. They were right, and I did my best to remember the cost to persons as over against the cost to projects.

Of course the Oriental Institute survived. It survived because of a valued program and a dedicated staff. The younger scholars had come from the United States, Canada, and Europe to be Orientalists at a research institution. They buckled down to their jobs with groans but without revolt, and they did their work under the new conditions. Indeed, adversity made the young people, husbands and wives, a very cohesive group. We played badminton and softball together and had gay evenings playing parlor games. Three or four of the senior professors were feuding with one another. When we observed this, we were confident that our common dedication and mutual trust would never permit us to descend to such personal malevolence. (And so, if later we had our own sharp differences, we would claim that we were standing on high principle rather than personal ambition, not recognizing that our seniors had made the same claim.) Between the financial disaster of 1936 and the preoccupation with the Second World War, there was an admirable spirit among the institute scholars. They worked and played hard together, and they served Oriental studies faithfully.

There were certain things that a young administrator could do. When Elisha did assume the mantle of Elijah, he found that he had to be himself and not attempt to be the titanic Elijah. With fewer projects in the field, with a smaller staff, it was possible to deal in terms of persons. Instead of summoning scholars to my office, I could go to theirs and listen to them with unflagging patience. The courtesy of full communication was not a substitute for a better salary and wide research opportunity, but it did give the feeling of a shared problem.

It was also now possible to introduce democratic deliberation into the scholarly community. In the older University of Chicago eminent scholars had run their own departments by imperial fiat. Even in the 1930s a forum for discussion of policy and common decision was not conspicuous at the university. Now meetings of the institute and of the department became more frequent and dealt with general policy. Everyone could be heard and could vote. After one departmental meeting, a young instructor smilingly said that he had never attended a more interesting seminar. Certainly communication and mutual responsibility help any institution.

Two of my seniors, Harold Nelson and William A. Irwin, were unfailingly sympathetic and unobtrusively helpful. I had been told that he who became an administrator lost his friends, but this proved to be false. With most of the excavations closed down, we found that ideas could be more exciting than new objects. When Frankfort finished his digging in Iraq and came to teach at the university, his untiring curiosity and his productive imagination fired others with a happy sense that they also were vigorous pioneers on important frontiers. There were advantages within poverty.

How vigorous those years were may be seen by a selection of Oriental Institute publications (all issued by the University of Chicago Press). *Ancient Egyptian Paintings* (1936), by Nina M. Davies and Alan H. Gardiner, was a sumptuous offering. Pinhas Delougaz' *The Temple Oval at Khafajah* (1940) clarified early Babylonian temple architecture. Gordon Loud's *The Megiddo Ivories* (1939) presented exciting little carvings found in Palestine. Robert J. Braidwood's *Mounds in the Plain of Antioch: an Archaeological Survey* (1937) was a model study of a little-known area. Henri Frankfort's *Sculpture of the Third Millennium B.C. from Tell Asmar and Khafajah* (1939) was a study of early Babylonian sculpture marked by great insight. George G. Cameron completed a book by the late Edward Chiera, *They Wrote on Clay: the Babylonian Tablets Speak Today* (1938), a popular work that still has a lively sale today. Other valuable publications were appearing at the same time, but these few will give an index of the vigorous outpourings of active minds.

The Second World War eliminated most field activity, and most of the younger staff were drawn into some kind of government service. These factors so reduced the annual budgets between 1942 and 1946 that the institute accumulated an unexpected small surplus. When the fighting was over it seemed worth while for me to go out to the Near East to assess the postwar possibilities for field work.

Just before Christmas 1945 I left Washington on an Army Transport plane. The trip out at that season of the year was an adventure. After we had been snowed in for a night at Stephenville, Newfoundland, we set out across the wintry Atlantic. In about three hours the plane suddenly turned around and started back. We had been heading for the Azores, and the control tower there had been blown down by a storm. Now the pilot wanted to find any airport between New York and Newfoundland. Later the passengers learned that a blizzard had set in along the American coast, so that no airfield in Canada or the United States would take the responsibility of receiving us. The captain of the plane was on his own. He decided to return to Stephenville, came in through blinding snow, banked sharply, leveled off, and made a perfect landing. Only after we were safely down did we find out how tense the situation had been in the cockpit.

It took us nearly five days to go from Washington to Cairo. The passengers were a mixed bag of the military, foreign-service officers, and oil men. A burly chief petty officer, who had taken the dangerous crossing of the Atlantic Ocean as a normal risk, gripped the arms of his seat when we flew over the Atlas Mountains between Casablanca and Tripoli, glared out of the window, and growled, "This ain't safe! They oughtn't to fly over mountains like this!" At dawn on Christmas Day we flew over the ghastly wreckage on the battlefield of El-Alamein, dipped down to salute the pyramids at Gizah, and landed in Cairo.

Harold Nelson was back at Chicago House in Luxor, but it was impossible to reach him by telephone. Nor did I succeed in finding any of my Cairo friends at home. An oil man and I sat down to a somber Christmas dinner, remembered our families at home, looked at each other, and gave an ironic toast to a Merry Christmas.

In Egypt it was clear that the Epigraphic Survey could continue at Luxor, but otherwise the atmosphere was obscure. The Antiquities Service had gone through a bad experience of discovering that monuments had been systematically looted for some years, particularly at Thebes. Great chunks had been cut out of the walls of tombs for clandestine sale in Cairo. There was a sense of frustration and guilt that nothing had been done about it. The reaction was to blame somebody else for something else. The Keeper of the Cairo Museum recited the list of American institutions that had received loans of objects for study and that had never returned them. For example, the Oriental Institute had ostraca, scraps of stone or pottery with writing (hieratic, demotic, Coptic, and Greek), which had been turned up in clearing the area around the temple of Medinet Habu. The implication was that we would not be welcome until we brought back those loans.

Archaeology has always been affected by national pride. A few years later I called upon an old Egyptian friend, who was now Deputy Minister of Education. His greeting was, "Your American Army had the head of Nefert-iti in your hands at the end of the war, and you did not give it back to us in Egypt!" It was futile for me to protest that the Army's Fine Arts Commission was not permitted to go back earlier than the depredations of Mussolini or Göring in returning treasures to their former owners. Where Nefert-iti—or her husband Akh-en-Aton or any other members of the Amarna family, for that matter—is concerned, emotions fly out the window and common sense follows.

In that winter of 1946 some Army people whom I had known in Washington were crossing from Cairo to Baghdad by motorcar. They invited me to join them. It proved to be a chancy trip, as we had constant car trouble, always out in some cold, uninhabited stretch of desert. In traveling through four countries we went through seven frontier or military check points. My friends had military passes, which covered them, a wife, and a servant. But I had an ordinary passport, which described me as an "archaeologist." This puzzled the officials at every check point. Why was a colonel of the American Army driving a civilian who claimed to be an archaeologist? At the Suez frontier a British officer suggested that I be put under military orders in order to cross Sinai into Palestine. A document was drawn up placing me under the command of my friend, Colonel Hudson. At the Iraq frontier a British sergeant was detailed to question me. Since he obviously knew nothing about archaeology, it was difficult for him to determine whether I really was an archaeologist. I answered that, no, I had never dug at Babylon; no, I had never dug at Damascus. He ran out of places and then had to invent the names of some alleged British archaeologists. Did I know Smith, Jones, or Brown? I had to confess that I had never heard of them. In this negative way I passed the test, and we were allowed to proceed.

In Baghdad I was invited to a luncheon at the American Legation. Another guest was the scholar who was serving as Oriental Secretary for the British Embassy. Apparently he had never heard of me, because he treated me with cold caution. Then at one point he used the phrase "his ever-loving wife," and I pounced on this. It turned out that we were both enthusiasts for Damon Runyon's stories about the shady characters along Broadway. He warmed up immediately. I believe that I passed a test as an Orientalist because I had read some fables about tawdry life in New York City.

Iraq was the most promising of the five countries visited. The Director-General of Antiquities, Naji el-Asil, was cordial and intelligent. Two young Iraqis who had taken masters' degrees at Chicago were among his assistants, and Seton Lloyd, an Englishman formerly of our Iraq dig, was an adviser. The director-general gave a picnic in my honor at the ruined ziggurat of Aqar Quf, the Babylonian Temple tower twenty miles east of Baghdad. A poem in classical Arabic commemorating this glorious occasion was read. It seemed that I might assure our people at home that they would be welcome in Iraq.

Before I had left Chicago I had talked with the highest administrative officials of the university about the future of the Oriental Institute. They had expressed a kindly interest in my mission and had given me the impression that I could be away for three months with no worries. One month later, while I was in Luxor, a letter arrived informing me that the trustees had exercised their right to take over for the general purposes of the university the money that the Rockefeller boards had assigned to the Oriental Institute in 1936 for a period of ten years. This letter, perhaps through clerical inadvertence, had been sent to me by ordinary surface mail. It had been written only a few days after I left Chicago. I promptly cabled back a protest at this "arbitrary" action and submitted my resignation as director.

The situation was charged with emotion. Even after twenty-five years it is difficult to treat it objectively. The $2,000,000, if treated as if it were endowment, had permitted the institute to live within its income. If the institute now had to seek support from the university administration or from outside, its freedom would be limited. Yet one could sympathize with trustees who had the responsibility of building up the general assets of a university. There was hurt pride in the knowledge that the administration had not prized the institute as an outstanding research institution and so had not maintained its financial integrity. Of course my personal pride was wounded. There had been a lack of communication between the administration and the institute. I could have been advised of the contingency before I left Chicago. This rather formal announcement sent by slow mail seemed very deliberate.

When I returned to Chicago in the spring I reiterated my resignation, to take effect as soon as a successor was found. The protest by my colleagues was heart-warming. The official reason for my resignation was that I wanted to return to teaching and research, which was true enough. It was in any case the time to resign. If I had exceeded those ten or eleven years as director, I might have gone on indefinitely, which was not good for any institution. Further, I had accomplished my work of financial retrenchment, and the administration may have felt that there should be a more positive leadership.

In his Chancellor's Annual Report for 1946, Robert M. Hutchins was both generous in his words about me and realistic in appraising my restricted leadership. "John A. Wilson, Professor of Egyptology, who has been director of the Oriental Institute for the past eleven years, has given up his administrative duties to give his time to those of his professorship. Mr. Wilson gave an admirable account of himself in the days when the budget of the Institute had to be reduced from more than $600,000 a year to less than $200,000. He held the Institute together, preserved the essentials of its work, and enabled it to retain its position as one of the leading centers of Near Eastern studies in the world. Thorkild Jacobsen, Oriental Institute Professor of Social Institutions, and a member of the Institute for eighteen years, has been appointed Director."

It is a commentary on the attitudes of the faculty at an American university that I received more approbation from my colleagues in other departments for resigning from administrative office than I had ever received for accepting such office.

NINE

WASHINGTON

As the Second World War ground on in Europe and American involvement seemed inevitable, several of the Oriental Institute scholars began to prepare themselves for government service. Those who dealt with ancient languages had experience with decipherment and enrolled in the course on cryptography offered by the Army Signal Corps. Codes and decoding fascinated me, and I studied eagerly for some months. However, destiny had other plans for me.

In Washington, Colonel William Donovan had organized an intelligence agency, now remembered under its second name, the Office of Strategic Services, or OSS. The agency had several branches. I learned almost nothing about the cloak-and-dagger field work, because the tight security surrounding it seemed entirely appropriate to those who worked on the other side. As I shall explain, I joined that other side. We belonged to the Research and Analysis Branch, headed by William L. Langer, professor of European History at Harvard. Our part of that branch was the Division of Special Information, located in the Library of Congress. We focused on the books and journals of the Library and on the more general reports from the field. We read newspapers and statistical reports from foreign countries and studied such intelligence reports as were not withheld from us as Top Secret. The chief qualifications for this research were field experience and a knowledge of foreign languages. For many parts of the world the United States lacked experts who could think in terms of strategic thrust. For Asia and Africa the staff was constructed out of the few professional regional experts, and then was padded with those who had taught in foreign countries, archaeologists, missionaries, and linguists. It was decidedly an amateur group that faced the hard-boiled problems of war.

A few weeks after the attack on Pearl Harbor, I was asked to come to Washington by my friend of Beirut days, Walter L. Wright, Jr. He was the chief of that research group working in the Library of Congress. He had to return to his position as president of Robert College in Turkey, and he invited me to take over his position in Washington. Under the urgent conditions of January 1942, the transfer of functions went through very rapidly. Washington officials were so hard pressed that I was working on confidential documents some weeks before my security clearance came through. The University of Chicago gave me a leave of absence. Harold Nelson and Henri Frankfort generously took over my administrative duties.

Before my new appointment—as Chief of the Division of Special Information of the Research and Analysis Branch of the Coordinator of Information, as well as Chief of the Near East Section of the division—was final, I was commuting between Chicago and Washington on those overworked railroad trains of wartime. The capital was already overcrowded, but five young Orientalists invited me to share their flat near the Library of Congress. That took care of my lodging for the first nine months of 1942. Mary and the children stayed on in Chicago for the school year and until I could find a place for a family of five. I finally bought a little house in College Park, Maryland, and they joined me in the autumn. The Baltimore and Ohio's commuter trains brought me within a few blocks of the Library of Congress every morning.

Our division at the Library then numbered about one hundred and twenty persons, and our field was the world. Some members of the staff were already distinguished, like Conyers Read, professor of English history at the University of Pennsylvania, and W. Norman Brown, professor of Indic Studies at the same institution. Others have since risen to high distinction—Ralph Bunche of the United Nations, and John K. Fairbank, professor of Chinese History at Harvard.

The group was not bureaucratic, nor was it power-seeking. There was a job to be done, to learn more about Latin America, Europe, Africa, and Asia. Into that work went such chores as studying the reports from Japanese navy yards, identifying personalities in the Syrian independence movement, and reading newspapers written in Uzbek. How much chrome was being shipped out of Turkey, and to whom did the shipments go? Would it be possible to send a shipload of coffee to Turkey and thereby win some gratitude for the United States? What was that mysterious and powerful figure, el-Glaoui, doing about the Moroccan independence party? Where were General Leclerc's Free French forces last reported in Africa? Who in the world authorized the shipping of sand to Saudi Arabia for the building of an airport? What other country might use the broad-gauge railroad equipment intended for a destination taken over by the enemy?

I set myself to study the Egyptian Delta. If Rommel broke through at el-Alamein, could the Germans cross the Delta rapidly? There were no through roads there, and the network of small local railroads led to no important destinations. There was hardly a problem that was not pertinent. We knew nothing about psychological warfare, but we did know something about the psychology of foreign peoples. A propaganda booklet planned by the Office of War Information seemed to us shock-ingly inappropriate for Asia and Africa. Pictures of an American supermarket or of American teenagers walking along hand in hand and laughing would have no appeal or no comprehension in Egypt or Iran, and we said so. On the other hand, everybody would be attracted by the picture of a small boy writing in class, and we said so. When I visited my "opposite number" in Army Intelligence, I found him equipped with a map of the Near East, put out by the *National Geographic Magazine*, with no refer-ence to strategic considerations. He talked about the "Ay-rabs" as though they were all primitive nomads. All of this was very new to us, and we went at it with tireless energy and a deter-mined optimism.

We were perfectly willing to put in a nine-hour day at the office and then work evenings and weekends. We needed to take material home to study in off time, but the Library of Congress had its long-standing rules. Our division wanted a relaxation of those rules. We had a difficult session with the librarian, who told us plainly that his responsibility was to materials under his care and that we would not be permitted to use them or the library in any arbitrary fashion. We felt he was insensitive to our exceptional needs. We did not win our point but we went on trying.

Bureaucracy said that all desks should be parallel to the wall or at right angles to the wall. One scholar insisted that he could work only with the light coming in from the window at an angle over his shoulder. I told him to get on with the job and put his desk at any angle he wanted. Efficiency experts looked us over and decreed that, for the proper dispatch of the day's problems, every desktop should be clear of papers at the end of each day. We simply shoveled the papers into a drawer, which looked neater but only added to the confusion. Another expert's idea of compact efficiency was to shelve all books by size first and by color second. We ignored that.

We were proud of our research unit. We went after and

found the best materials available in Washington or commandeered them from elsewhere. Bureaucratic rules were bypassed. If we wanted to send a situation report to another agency, it had to be typed in quadruplicate and sent through channels, which might take four days. It was quicker to have it typed in quintuplicate and then carry one copy across town and deliver it personally to the addressee. Much vital information could not go into writing and had to be transmitted orally. It was alleged that one way to give or get something was to attend a cocktail party and get off in a corner with some key man. I found this too risky and too expensive of energy to be of much use.

Three or four of us lived out in College Park, and in wintertime we were away from dark to dark. Early one morning before Christmas 1943, we reached the little suburban station as the train pulled in. We scrambled aboard, stopped in the door of the car, and burst into laughter. The railroad had been so short of rolling stock under holiday pressure that cars that went well back into the nineteenth century had been dug out. The coach had a long bench down the middle, benches against each wall, a pot-bellied stove, and dim, antiquated electric bulbs. We were always deadly serious about getting to work each morning. It was good of the railroad to afford us a little comic relief.

My day began in the air-conditioned Library of Congress. After about three hours I usually took a bus across town to OSS headquarters, which were not air-conditioned. I would come back to the library for the final two hours of the day. In the cold sleet of winter or the steaming heat of summer this change of atmosphere was exhausting. For the most part I was too grimly intent on the next step to notice where I was. But there were occasional spring days, when the sun broke through and the forsythia suddenly blossomed, when I looked out of the window of the bus and exclaimed to myself, "What a beautiful city!"

If this account suggests gaiety and gusto in the work, that has to be understood in a setting of oppressive urgency and frustration. Every one of us was myopically intent on winning the war, but the war dragged on despite our efforts. Those days seem now like the memory of a restless dream. My own performance fell far short of my hopes. Research about fact was something that a scholar understood. The application of knowledge for immediate power purposes was something for which scholars were not adapted. Psychological warfare or that unknown hush-hush side of OSS involved attitudes and techniques outside the normal range of an academic mind. I did not have the discipline for ruthless purpose.

Washington often ignored our precision as being inconsequential. When a young Army officer briefed us about the situation near el-Alamein he kept referring to the Qattara Depression as "the Quarter-ah Depression." I went up to him afterward and said, "That depression is Qattara, pronounced like catarrh-ah." He nodded his acknowledgment. Next week he resumed his report about activity around "the Quarter-ah Depression." Americans often have a little scorn for the professor who has knowledge but "does not know much."

The dogmatic thrust that was a necessary part of the government setting was beyond me, though it was surely justified. Nobody could be heard in that frantically busy setting unless he spoke out loudly and confidently. It was a naïve hope that good work would speak for itself, without a loud and repeated assertion that it was the best. My diffidence applied even to making a budget. When I estimated the probable costs for the coming six months, I put down a 20-per-cent increase in personnel as being about all that we could use. It would be difficult even to find twenty-five more persons who had the necessary qualifications, and we could not break in much more than that number. A telephone call came through asking me to demand more. When I explained the basis of the estimate, I was told that our work was so important that we should show a really forceful claim for more. The estimated increase was raised to 33 per cent. This brought, not a request, but a brusque order to go much higher. I asked for a 60-per-cent raise. We finally got about 25 per cent. Since I did not understand this jockeying for position, since I did not travel from office to office emphasizing our discoveries, my division probably suffered in competition with others. I knew how to operate within university politics, where the characteristic attack has the stylized formula of fencing, but not under the saturation bombing in Washington.

There was a popular suspicion that many archaeologists served as government spies. Even though the cloak-and-dagger activities of OSS were kept secret from us on the research side, I was aware that there was some such use during the Second World War. Before that time and since that time I have known of no archaeologists serving as government agents. They really have two liabilities against such employment. Their professional concern is for the ancient, and if they should show a visible curiosity about the modern this would be very conspicuous. Secondly, they normally pursue their archaeology in some desert or rural setting, where there simply is no strategic information to be gained. Few archaeologists have more than a superficial knowledge of the obscure power forces in the countries where they work.

The Free French had taken Syria and Lebanon and were well settled there. The Allies had won el-Alamein and had begun driving the enemy back across north Africa. The pressure on the Near East had relaxed. After eighteen months with OSS, I transferred in July 1943 to the Cultural Relations Office of the Department of State. At the risk of sounding sanctimonious, I must say that I hoped to understand cultural factors better than I had understood warfare. The American program of cultural exchanges with Latin America had made some headway. It was now proposed to extend such relations to Africa and Asia. Perched on a height across the street from the old State Department was an old building that had once been the home of General Grant. On the top floor I sat with my staff: one person for North Africa, one for the Arab world, one for Turkey, and one for India. Our specific task was to find and send out cultural relations officers to the American delegations in our area. We hoped our people would be well received, but there were incidents that clouded our optimism. One day the Minister to Turkey came in and demanded to know whether this new officer would take precedence over the military or naval attachés in a reception line or in table seating. When he was told that a new man could expect no precedence, he said, "That's all I wanted to know! If he keeps out of my way, I won't interfere with him!" Once more we did not seem to enjoy warm acceptance in professional circles.

We sent out libraries of American books to various cities in the world, brought art exhibits to this country, encouraged the development of the drama in Iran, and started a modest program for the exchange of foreign and American scholars. The program was small, but we believed that intellectual communities provided a yeast in their countries, so that it would be helpful both to us and to them if these were encouraged and assisted. I dreamed up a massive program to foster village arts and crafts, so that they might survive against the competition of machine-made goods. It came to nothing. It is not enough to support the local artisans; you have to set up market outlets for their goods and to advertise their superior qualities. This was too much for us.

One small working team was enjoying such adventures that the stenographer said that she wished that she too had an area for cultivation. I solemnly assigned her Trucial Oman for study. She was surprised to find that there was such a place. To be sure, at that time it was not easy to work out a program of cultural exchange between the trucial sheikhdoms on the east coast of Arabia and the United States.

In 1944 I was summoned back to the University of Chicago to try to build up a program of regional studies. The war had shown the universities that there was a real need for specialists on various parts of the world. My attempt failed. Regional programs involve cooperation among different departments. At that time no department was willing to sacrifice some of its independence in order to do something quite new. The chairman of the Geography Department told me that there was no need for studies of world areas, because Geography was already doing that. Departments specializing in foreign languages were unwilling to lower their requirements in order to accommodate students from the social sciences, and in the Division of Social Sciences only History and Anthropology were mildly interested. It would be nearly twenty years before the university would set up interdepartmental programs in African, Middle Eastern, South Asian, and other regional studies.

The work of my expansively named Committee on World Affairs was thus premature. Perhaps that was just as well. None of us as yet had worked out the problems of interdepartmental relations sufficiently to be persuasive. There was a defeat even within the Oriental Institute, when a majority of the voting members went on record as being concerned with ancient times and opposing any attempt to "dilute" such concentration by the introduction of modern studies. What hurt more than anything else was the charge that such changes would "betray the memory" of James Henry Breasted. If I knew the man, such studies would have excited his ever eager imagination. Change was slow, and there was no new legislative action; but we now take a concern for the modern as appropriate.

For nearly a year I shuttled back and forth between Chicago and Washington. For two or three days each week I was with the Department of State for the cultural relations work. After American interests in Africa and Asia had warmed up somewhat, this part-time service was unsatisfactory, and supervision of the cultural program was taken over by Colonel William A. Eddy, who had been born in the Near East and who had had a distinguished academic and diplomatic career. Later, when I saw the busy American libraries in Near Eastern cities and when I participated in the Fulbright program, I was proud to have been a part of this program, which, in its purest form, was independent of power politics and was concerned with people and ideas.

TEN

⬥⬥⬥⬥⬥⬥⬥⬥⬥

FAMILY

IT IS fortunate that my wife Mary likes to travel. She comes by that honestly on both sides of her family. Maternal ancestors were Maine ship captains, who carried ice to Calcutta, brought back guano from Peru, and took warming pans to Jamaica for puddling molasses. The household had tales and souvenirs from distant lands. Her father was a liberal Congregationalist minister, whose delight was to explore frontier rivers in Canada. He had different parishes, so that Mary can happily claim Maine, Nebraska, or Wisconsin as her home state. Her mother's family always looked up reverently to Boston. The psychology is planetary: forever orbiting and yet always drawn toward a central focus. Thus she has been able to construct a warm, attractive home in Chicago, even though we may often be away. For children that reliable point of return is very important.

If I should claim that our two older children were born while I was up a ladder in Egypt, that is only a slight exaggeration of the truth. In 1928 and in 1930 Mary came back from Egypt to await the arrival of Margaret, known as Peggy, and of Frederick Thomas, known as Tom, while I continued work with the Epigraphic Survey at Luxor. So I was not in attendance until Constance arrived in 1933.

In preparation for the birth of our first child Mary was staying with her sister Winnie in Massachusetts. Dan Bliss and I worked out an elaborate code to notify me out in Egypt. Each of us had a copy of a commercial code book, and we inserted all of the possibilities we could think of. For example, we might have crossed out "sell if market rises" for CRWHM and inserted "girl," or crossed out "750 pounds sterling" for MPKRT and inserted "seven pounds, five ounces." Thus a cablegram of only a few coded words could carry a lot of information. I was up a ladder at Medinet Habu, collating a scene on the north wall, when one of our artists appeared, shouting at me and waving a cablegram. My code book was back at Chicago House, ten minutes away. Without it the cryptogram was impossible. I do not remember coming down the ladder, but I was back at the house in less than ten minutes. The news was good, but Dan and I agreed that the cable would be in plain English the next time.

In celebration of Peggy's birth I gave the servants at Chicago House a sheep for their feasting. They were inclined to sympathize with me that the first-born had not been a boy. Mahmud, our room man, assured me that girls could be useful around the house and might be married off to advantage. He probably thought that my joy was simply putting the best face on a disappointment. Two years later, when Tom arrived, the servants must have thought that a boy should mean a bigger gift than the one sheep given for a girl. Before I had taken any action, they came to me and said that there had been some quarreling about the choice cuts taken from the previous animal; this time they would like the money for the sheep (plural) instead of the beast itself. Perhaps my esteem with them went down when I gave them the money to cover only a single animal.

The three children grew up in Chicago, with vacations at the family home in Connecticut while I taught summer school. Their schooling began in the University Nursery School when they were only three. The education in the University of Chicago Laboratory School—nursery, kindergarten, elementary, and high school—was excellent. Yet it had a certain hot-house character in its experimentation with children from highly literate families. It was good for the children to go to public school while we were in Washington during the war, so that they had a taste of the democratic system at work. Whether in Chicago or in Washington, all three developed a strong social conscience. The two girls expressed this by going to Antioch College, where education is illustrated by the laboratory test of work away from the campus. Tom expressed it by going to a Quaker college and then becoming a pediatrician.

The children had a mother, but only part of a father. In my first years of teaching I was abstractedly intent on doing a better job in class. I came home only to sit down with books. When I took on the administration of the Oriental Institute, my preoccupation was even greater. I went to the office on weekends and was away traveling quite often. When I joined the family in Connecticut for the month of September, they had been at home there for two months and treated me as a short-time visitor. It may have been in the late 1930s that I came home to the evening meal in an unusually relaxed mood, made some small jokes, and showed an interest in the affairs of others. Tom said to his mother, "What's Dad feeling so good about tonight?" It came as a shock to me that I had been an absentee father.

The chance to join the family came in 1939. The plan had been that I should go to the Near East about the first of September, with the first goal a visit to Persepolis before that excavation closed for the season. I went to New York to sail on the *Normandie*. The day before sailing time, Germany invaded Poland, and the Second World War started. The ill-fated *Normandie* canceled her sailing and ultimately died at her New York dock. No alternative would bring me to Persepolis in time, and the

European situation was ominous. The trip was called off, and I sent a telegram to Mary in Chicago: what about a family vacation in that New Mexico place that friends had recommended so highly?

Before the First World War the Phelps Dodge Company had opened up a copper mine at Tyrone in southwestern New Mexico. It was a beautiful mountain setting, and the company decided that this should be no tin-shack mining town. They engaged a distinguished architect to design a model village, with adobe cottages in pastel colors grouped around the rims of the hills. There was a central plaza, with a town hall, post office, railroad station, and department store in the same gracious architecture. There was a well-equipped hospital. The place had charm. After that war the market for copper declined to a point where the mine had to be closed down. It was decided to rent the cottages to families who could stay for two weeks or more.

We started off immediately by motorcar. The discovery of the West was a family experience. Mary and I knew Europe and the Near East, but we had not motored across the wide prairies or paused in the majestic Rockies. The children had grown up in flat Chicago and knew only the gracious little hills of Connecticut. Suddenly we all had the common excitement of unlimited horizon. From our cottage we could see mountain peaks eighty miles away.

Except for the cryptography lessons I was doing under the Signal Corps, I was free to be with the family. We kept the swimming pool open into October, when it was too cool for anyone else. Nearby was a corral where we could rent riding horses. Fred Ramsey, the dude wrangler, was a delightful character who loved children. Never mind that the horses were so old that they had been retired to the job of plodding over mountain trails with a child or a cautious easterner; we came to regard them with affectionate trust. Once we were even allowed to participate in a cattle roundup, preliminary to sorting and branding. There was a picnic in a mountain spot more than a hundred miles away, which was a routine trip in these open spaces. This place had freedom and peace, a whole world away from the war clouds of Europe.

Tyrone itself was a ghost town. The department store looked as though it had just been closed for the night. There were still wires running from the sales counters up to a cashier's desk on the mezzanine. There were still those little cylindrical boxes to. carry money on the wires up to the cashier, so that he could make change and write a receipt. In the hospital the clipboards were still hanging on a rack, as though the doctors might be back at any moment, and a wheelchair was standing in the corridor. In the hospital washroom there was an authentic ghost-town touch. One of the toilets had a closed door, with its sign reading OCCUPIED.

The children so loved the western atmosphere that in self-defense I began to slough off my character as an effete easterner and pretend that I too had ridden the range at some distant time.

They would ask, "Daddy, what's that door back there in that hill?"

"That?" I would summon my resources. "Oh, that's where Old Man Woodward used to keep his blasting powder."

"Blasting powder! What for?"

Then I would work my way into character. "Oh, that was 'way back yonder, afore you was even breeched, when I was ridin' with the Woodward outfit, and we was puttin' the roadway through over towards Silver. Had to do a powerful lot of blastin' and blowin' and bustin', and that's no deception. So Old Man Woodward, so's to be safe and all, he tunneled back into that hill there and kept the blastin' powder way back insides."

"Was it dangerous?" They did not really believe my tale but were happy to go along with the game.

"Dangerous! Why, there must have been sixty, seventy barrels of blastin' powder way back into there, all set to go off if some kid nearby so much as sneezed. We had to keep the sneezin' kids pent up in a corral down the draw a piece."

"Oh, not really!"

"All right, so you don't believe me. Well, look—you see that kind of a hole up there in that tree a-standin' in front of the hillside, the place where there's no leaves nor branches up there a piece from the ground?"

They would locate the gap in the tree's foliage and wait for more.

"Well," I would say in triumph, "that proves it! 'Cause that's where Loco Billy gone through! Tunnel back there in that hill is long and straight like the barrel onto a shotgun. Seems that Loco Billy gone in there one day, and bein' kind of loco, like his name said, he carelesslike lit him a cigarette. Blastin' powder gone off and blew him plumb out of the tunnel like a shot out of a shotgun. He gone clean through that tree and ripped open that hole in the tree you can see there with your own eyes. Guess maybe you'll believe me after this!"

Somewhat impressed, they would ask, "Daddy, what happened to Loco Billy?"

"Oh, me and the other hands poked around over there a piece acrost the draw, and we was able to pick up the copper studs off of his Levis. I got some of them amongst my tack, if you was a mind to see them some time."

Thus was born the fictional character of Johnny, a former cowhand, now too old and "broke down" to do more than water the stock, mend harness, and spin tales for children.

We did our own housekeeping at Tyrone, and Mary had to wrestle with a cranky cooking stove, which consumed juniper, pine, and mahogany. She put the children to doing the day's dishes. They evaded this work unless they got a "Johnny story." Many of the tales had a moralistic value, like Johnny's righteous indignation against cowhands who drank too much Dr. Pepper or 7-Up, or against the hand who had to be isolated in the bunkhouse because he had the nasty habit of chewing bubble gum.

Before the Second World War cut short such vacations, we spent three Septembers in New Mexico. A new story every day became a desperate challenge. During the second and third vaca-

tions I had to go back and retell stories from a previous year
("No, Daddy, that wasn't the way it went!") or work in some
Bible stories, in which the Patriarchs were put into the setting of
the American frontier. Old Man Noah of the ARK outfit became
a foresighted farmer who introduced contour plowing against
the dangers of flooding. Jacob had to be excused for being only
a sheepherder: "Land wasn't rightly worth a bitty piece of
fencin' wire. Fellow couldn't take stock onto a range like that,
all broke up with dry arroyos and rocky mesas. Old Jake just
naturally had to run sheep onto scrubby land like that was, poor
feller!" Judge Solomon turned out to be a canny horse trader,
very stately and polite, but too shrewd to be caught in the
clutches of the widow woman Sheba.

These stories and later ones that involved the adventures of
grandchildren were strictly for family consumption and were
never committed to publication. A psychiatrist might question
the motives that led an Egyptologist to cast himself in the role
of an old cowboy. I might plead that it was an attempt to understand the American frontier, similar to my attempt to understand
the ancient Egyptian past. That explanation might have some
truth, even though it is casuistic. More penetrating might be the
question whether this bent toward tall fiction is reflected in my
supposedly serious historical writings. That might unconsciously
be the case; critics have called my descriptions of the ancient
Egyptians "speculative."

Mary and I had hoped that a time would come when we might
go out to the Near East as a family, so that the children might
see where I had worked. The Second World War prevented
that. By the time the struggle was over they were too deeply involved in their education to take time out. All three made happy
marriages and have their own children. The families are dispersed from the Atlantic to the Pacific coasts, so that visits by
grandparents have to be planned well in advance.

When anthropologists ask Egyptologists about kinship patterns, marriage systems, or social mobility, we are often embar-

rassed that we know so little that is consistent and significant. Therefore I set down here the evidence on our own children. Peggy married a Philadelphia Quaker engineer. They spent the first two years of married life on a Friends Service project in India. That had some reflection of the commitment of Mary and myself, going to Beirut as young people. Connie married a sociologist from San Francisco. She and her husband both studied that subject at Columbia University, unconsciously following the footsteps of my father in that respect. Tom provides the most interesting case for a kinship pattern. He married a Bliss from Beirut, the niece of his mother's brother-in-law. Although no blood relationship was involved, this certainly brought into play the common background and common interests of a clan.

The three children grew up taking ancient Egypt for granted, not as a matter for special interest. Now ancient Egypt constantly inserts itself into the school curriculum of the grandchildren, who believe that the field of their grandfather has some importance.

John A. Wilson, 1969

Waterside, the family home at Sherman, Connecticut, about 1927

John A. Wilson in 1911

The Wilson family, New York City, autumn 1918: *left to right, front row*—Margaret M., Pauline (Lane), Agnes; *back row*—Warren, Julius, John (Underwood & Underwood)

Chicago, 1950: Constance, Mary (Rouse), Thomas, John, Margaret L. (photograph by Mildred Mead)

Campus of the American University of Beirut, 1920: the Observatory at left, College Hall at right, Mount Sunnin in the background

Daniel Bliss and "Ozymandias," 1922. The fallen statue of Ramses II, now in the Ramesseum, was the inspiration for Shelley's sonnet

Chicago House staff and visitors, about 1926: *front row—center*, Edward DeLoach, *right*, Adriaan de Buck; *left to right, second row*—Caroline Ransom Williams, Uvo Hölscher, Harold H. Nelson, James H. Breasted, Clarence Fisher, Alan H. Gardiner, William F. Edgerton; *third row*—Robert Barr, Virgilio Canziani, Phoebe Byles, John A. Wilson, Mary R. Wilson, Alfred Bollacher

Carrying the manuscript of *Medinet Habu* away from Chicago House, Luxor, April 1928; in the car are Mary R. Wilson and the chauffeur Ilya

Collating at Medinet Habu with the boatswain's chair—face of the first pylon, spring 1930

Hermann Junker, George R. Reisner, James H. Breasted, and Ludwig Borchardt ·in the garden of the Continental Hotel, Cairo, 1935

The hills of western Thebes from Medinet Habu, looking northwest from the first
pylon across the Oriental Institute excavations, with the high mud-brick enclosure wall
in the middle distance

Archaeologists and officials of the Iraqi Service at the ziggurat of Aqar Quf, 1946: *left to right*—Iraqi official; Seton Lloyd, advisor to the Service; John A. Wilson; Naji el-Asil, director-general of the Service; Fuad Safar; Taha Baqir

At Harvard Camp, Gizah, 1946; looking east toward the Second Pyramid

Oriental Institute staff members with William F. Albright of The Johns Hopkins University, 1950: *left to right*—Hans G. Güterbock, Ignace J. Gelb, Albright, Benno Landsberger, Wilson, A. Leo Oppenheim, Thorkild Jacobsen

Henri Frankfort, Sir Leonard Woolley, and V. Gordon Childe, Cambridge, England, about 1950 (Robert Braidwood)

Receiving a medal and diploma from the Patriarch, as representative of the University of Chicago at the millennial of the Greek Patriarchal Library, Alexandria, 1952 (Vart, Istanbul)

The Chicago House staff with Egyptian officials at Deir el-Bahri, 1958: *left to right,
front row*—Mrs. Charles F. Nims, Charles F. Nims, Labib Habachi, Mary R. Wilson;
second row—Wilson, Reginald Coleman, Chief Inspector Mohammed Abd el-Qadir,
unknown official; *third row*—John Healey, Alexander Floroff, Fuad Yakub, Munir
Megally; *back row:* Salah Asman, Ibrahim Nawawi

With Her Majesty Queen Ingrid of Denmark in the Oriental Institute Museum, 1960, inspecting an Assyrian bull, c. 700 B.C., from the palace of Sargon at Khorsabad (*Chicago Tribune*)

Breaking ground at the Hierakonpolis excavation, 1967, with Gregory Possehl and workmen

Olf Klasens and Kazimierz Michalowski, east of the Small Temple
Abu Simbel, 1967

The Landscaping Group at Abu Simbel in 1968, looking down at the
Great Temple from the artificial hill over the Small Temple

Receiving a volume of dedicatory essays at his seventieth birthday party, Chicago, 1969

ELEVEN

COMMITTEE
MEMBER

WHEN I was appointed director of the Oriental Institute my name was little known outside the small world of Egyptology. Indeed it was hardly known inside the University of Chicago. President Hutchins, with—I hope—his tongue in his cheek, told the Board of Trustees that the appointment had been made because his father and my father had been classmates in college. After I had assumed the position there was some curiosity about the young man who had succeeded the great Breasted. I was considered for various committees having little to do with Oriental studies. On my part, I had a selfish reason for accepting committee membership, because I wanted to extend the limited contacts of the Oriental Institute. There began a thirty-year stretch in which I served with various groups for various causes. Within the university there were advisory and legislative councils, committees on university structure and professional ethics, editorial boards, and committees for fund-raising drives. Although my personal scholarship suffered by such activities, my new contacts were administratively useful. These and the calls from outside the university very greatly added to my education. At a considerable cost in time and effort, my own work gained a wider horizon.

When I was invited to serve on the governing board of the American Council of Learned Societies, I attended my first meeting with a proper sense of awe for the eminent scholars I was meeting there. The council serves as a clearinghouse and strategy board for the humanities. It is also the American representative of the International Union of Academies. Respectful silence should be the attitude of a freshman member. At the first luncheon the man sitting next to me asked, "Have you noticed that seven of the twelve men here part their hair on the right side?" He was a geographer, and I assumed that he was an expert on such topographic features. Since I part my hair on the right side, I understood that he was welcoming me to the fraternity. From that time forward I served with less diffidence. However, my service on committees was always more of a duty than an opportunity. Some years later, when I was on a subcommittee to revise the council's by-laws, critics of our sweeping proposals charged that the changes we proposed were attempts to seize power from the constituent societies and to vest that power in our own little cabal. The accusation that I might be interested in power always baffled me. Power means only added responsibility, and any new responsibility takes me away from the study of hieroglyphs, where I am happiest and most at home.

Another membership was pleasantly educational. A Chicago merchant, Charles R. Crane, had left a small endowment to create the Institute of Current World Affairs. The chief application of the funds was to enable young people to study little-known parts of the world. A Chicago colleague of mine had written an adverse review of a book on the Arabs published under the auspices of this institute. Since I was then chairman of department, the director of the Institute of Current World Affairs, Walter S. Rogers, came to me to protest the spirit and wording of that review. He was a superb interviewer, and our animated discussion ended by his inviting me to learn more about his foundation. One of the first meetings I attended was late in 1941. The talk centered on the invasion of Russia by Hitler's armies, with apparent sweeping success. There were three specialists on the Soviet Union present, and they agreed firmly that Russia could not be defeated by Germany and would end up victorious. At the time that seemed to be impossible, but it turned out to be a correct prophecy. It was an impressive example of regional expertness on problems little known to Americans. So I came into the governing body of the Institute of Current World Affairs and learned about such places as China, India, South Africa, and Argentina. The foundation invests in young people rather than in projects, and then gives them a relatively free hand to develop expertness in some area. The pleasure of this association was an acquaintance with regional specialists before such authorities were common in this country. Mr. Crane was a farsighted man.

I also went back to one of my old enthusiasms by becoming a trustee of the American University of Beirut. When I first knew it in 1920 it had been a good training school along American lines, usually staffed by people who were giving expression to a missionary urge. As the former missionary impulse has faded, the institution has been groping for some new quality of special service. It has gradually developed an appreciation of how important good research will be for the Near East. It has also slowly changed its education from a strictly American model, in order to fit the Near Eastern scene. Where the West pulls like a magnet it is not easy to stand firm on eastern soil. Twenty years ago an American philosopher visited the university and was baffled because the Arab teachers of philosophy wanted to talk about Whitehead and James and Babbitt, whereas he had been hoping to learn something about such Islamic philosophers as Ibn-Sina and al-Ghazali.

That experience would not be so true today. Whatever may be the attendant evils of nationalism, a pride in ancestral achievements has brought a greater interest in the learned past of the Near East. Similarly, research in the sciences at the university has produced knowledge that applies specifically to the area. Scholars there have produced a drought-resisting wheat adapted to the Near East and a baby food using cheap local plants. A study of the changing patterns of commercial fishing off the Phoenician coast has been undertaken because these waters have been affected by the new High Dam in Egypt. This research of quality gives great promise for the needs of the area. It owes a great deal to a fellow trustee, Professor Philip K. Hitti, the Arabist of Princeton. He has kept on insisting that the professors at Beirut must be scholars as well as teachers.

Within Oriental studies the changes over the past thirty years have been extraordinary. The field had been humanistic, philological, and classical. The American Oriental Society had a central core of learned men, most of them teaching in the universities along the northeast coast, with specialties in Biblical studies, classical Arabic, Sanskrit, or classical Chinese. Political history was taken for granted as a product of skill in the texts. There was little concern for cultural history, archaeology, the social sciences, or modern aspects of the Orient. After all, one could pick up enough of the colloquial language out in the field to transact the necessary business, and such distractions as the feminist movement in Egypt or the future of the British and French mandates in the Near East were better left to diplomats, merchants, and missionaries.

The administrative offices of the American Council of Learned Societies and of the Social Science Research Council foresaw the need for a knowledge of the modern Orient. They set up planning committees to recommend new trends in Oriental studies. These committees were of course made up of scholars who were currently active in universities. Quite honestly they could see how to advance the work they were doing more clearly than they could see how to experiment with the new. When proposals for change were laid before them, the committee members were sufficiently divided so that no action could be taken. I was as much at fault as any of the others. If I did have some vague feeling that a larger scope would be beneficial, I was myself a classicist and had no clearly organized idea of how to enlarge our understanding. The committee's chief contribution was a compilation of selections from Arabic texts—for students of the language.

The Second World War dramatically changed this static situation. The national need was for detailed knowledge of many cultures. It was not enough just to study Europe. We had to become familiar with Asia, Latin America, and ultimately Africa. The American Council of Learned Societies, prompted by the Linguistic Society of America, pioneered the rapid teaching of little-known modern languages. The method was somewhat startling to the traditionalists in the teaching of Oriental languages. The Linguistic Society had long experience in the study of languages with no writing, like those of the American Indian. It knew how to analyze such languages without referring to the framework of European syntax. The classicists were of course concerned with the old written languages. They demanded a two- or three-year term to teach them, using a grammatical approach, which ultimately derived from the teaching of Greek or Latin. Now under the demands of wartime, strange modern languages were taught in a few months. Emphasis was on the spoken language, without any necessary reference to the written. Western grammatical analysis was a distraction rather than a help in the dissection of Japanese or Tagalog or Swahili. It was a shock to hear the linguists say that they would prefer that the teacher of a language have no professional knowledge of it; he should approach it with the same open innocence as the students. Without preconceptions he would be freer to make his analysis and reconstruction. Native-born people could be found to give the correct pronunciation, but the teaching should be done by someone who knew language, even if not this particular language. If the traditionalists were shocked by this dismissal of slowly accumulated knowledge, they had to admit that the Army language schools showed that young Americans could have their tongues freed for strange languages in a remarkably short time.

Even more subversive for the older Orientalists was the invasion by the social sciences. The new regional studies meant a reorganization and reorientation of existing departments. The Department of Oriental Languages and Literatures, for example, taught the history of Islam with only a brief bow to modern trends. In order to characterize Islam, most of the time was spent upon its beginnings. The department expressed no interest in modern politics, economics, or sociology. For a long time it was not concerned with the modern literature of the Orient. In the social sciences, geography and anthropology did deal with foreign problems, but economics, sociology, and political science were firmly rooted in America and Europe. It was difficult for them to deal with a structure as different as the Asian or African, particularly when that meant competence in a strange language. Some history departments offered courses on India or China without teachers who could handle the languages of those regions. For any department the addition of new specialists meant budgetary competition for funds that were already in high demand. Until the big foundations like Ford and Rockefeller provided additional money, the young regionalists found difficulty in gaining appointments at the universities.

They also had difficulty in achieving full recognition within the professional societies. This was true in the social sciences, but the real breaking point came in the American Oriental Society. The older scholars who formed the governing group were usually committed to tradition. Certainly there should be concern about Arab nationalism, the split between India and Pakistan, or the spread of communism, but that should not change the teaching and research in Arabic, Chinese, or Sanskrit classics. Meetings of the society were heavily committed to papers on linguistic and philological problems of past cultures. Papers on the politics of modern Turkey or the folk customs of modern India were relatively few and had to be assigned to a smaller room on the second floor. When young regionalists protested the structure and procedure of the society, their protests were referred to the executive committee for consideration and recommendation. Even though that was proper legal procedure, it seemed like evasion to the young rebels.

Those who dealt with the modern Far East were the first to take action by forming their own society, which has become the Association for Asian Studies. It would not be correct to say that there was a divorce from the American Oriental Society, because many scholars have held membership in both societies. There was a separation, with each party living in its own apartment, the Association for Asian Studies on the busy ground floor and the American Oriental Society up in the quiet tower.

This pattern was successful and appealed to the younger scholars working on the modern Near East. They were slower in their attempt to reach community. By the time they felt strong enough to demand separate identity the big philanthropic foundations were supporting regional studies at the universities. The young specialists thought that such teaching would benefit if they had their own organization. Would some agency provide money so that they could form a professional society, with the costs covered for office overhead, a journal of their own, and meetings? I had to preside over a meeting at which a negative answer was given to this hope. Unless they were strong enough and determined enough to launch their own society with their own money, they would either fail or would be annual clients for outside support. Vitality had to come from inside. They did persist and did found their own association by their own efforts. These modernists talk the same language that we do, but theirs is a distinct dialect. Or perhaps theirs is the living and ours a dead language.

The interests of the humanist classicists are not diametrically opposed to those of the social science modernists. Both of us want to know about man. Recently a boy came to see me; he said that he wanted to study ancient Egypt but did not want any of "that old stuff" about verb forms and hymns to the gods. He wanted to go straight to the question of how the Egyptians lived. I rose rather truculently to this bait. Did he think that we old duffers were interested in grammar and not in people? Certainly we tried to make our translations of verb forms more precise, but that was because we wanted to get into the minds of the ancients. Certainly we translated hymns to the gods, because they showed the hopes and fears of a people who were intensely religious. But that was not all there was to it. One Egyptologist had analyzed the prices paid for barley, donkeys, and slaves, and had discovered a period of distressing inflation in the twelfth century B.C. Another was interested in how an ancient farmer purchased land and whether he then had a clear title to it. Another had discovered that poor people who had no sponsor on earth might write letters to the gods for help. In my own youth I had written an article about exhibitions of wrestling and single-stick before the king of Egypt and had speculated that the contests may have been staged performances instead of true contests, since the Egyptian was always shown as victorious over a foreign rival. It was news to the prospective student that some of those up in the ivory tower might have their field glasses trained on the scene down below.

What is now going on in Oriental studies may be called specialization or fragmentation, according to one's emotional bias. A similar process is visible inside the universities. At the University of Chicago the Department of Oriental Languages and Literatures recognized the necessity of a broader viewpoint and changed its name to Oriental Languages and Civilizations. With more numerous personnel available for the modern Orient and for eastern Asia, a Center for Middle Eastern Studies, a Department of Far Eastern Languages and Civilizations, and a Department of South Asian Languages and Civilizations have been set up. Our own department has contracted to Near Eastern Languages and Civilizations. Its strongest offerings continue to be ancient and medieval, but it has work in modern languages and history, and its offerings in history are broadly cultural. These are healthy trends. What was prematurely proposed back in 1944–45 has become a reality, although in sweeping terms that would have astonished me in those days.

Specialization means both refining and narrowing. The fragmentation of Oriental studies has strengthened the control of restricted fields of study at the cost of the broader picture. Narrowing down the focus cuts off the wider periphery of vision, which includes outside contacts. It is all very well to insist that a picture has more meaning if you can play light upon it from different directions. But life is short, and our immediate interests demand all of our time and attention.

In a presidential address before the American Oriental Society (*Journal of the American Oriental Society*, 1952) I gave my own wistful goals. "In relation to the central position of the pharaoh in ancient Egypt I might profit by a study of the cult of the Japanese emperor. To understand better the governmental bureaucracy under the Egyptian Empire I might gain useful insight by learning something about the civil service in China. I might understand the intricacies of Egyptian mythology better if I knew more about the avatars of an Indian deity. I might have a sharper picture of temple ritual if I knew the daily activities and the festival activities in a Ceylonese or Burmese temple at the present day. Modern analogies in India might give me useful ideas about the sacred character of ancient Egyptian animals. Perhaps a clearer understanding of the attitude of the Yezidis [the so-called devil worshipers] toward the devil would help me to understand the ancient Egyptian reconciliation of opposing forces into a single theological system."

Alas, I am still trying to keep abreast of my own narrow field and am still as ignorant of the analogies from other fields as I was then! Indeed, when cultures are so very different, any possible similarity is not easy to establish. A brief visit to the Far East and South Asia only increased the fogginess of the picture.

I was told firmly that all the Hindu divinities were expressions of a single god, no matter how divergent they might appear on the surface. That might have some relation to ancient Egyptian religion, but one would still have to distinguish in both cultures between theological dogma and the actual practice of worship. Theology says, "Only one god." Practice says, "This one god right now, without reference to all the others."

There are committees and committees. I once presided over an excellent committee composed of three college presidents and a dean. They were courteous but firm, businesslike yet imaginative, and they wanted to get the best job done in the minimum time. They did not have to impress other members of the committee by speeches establishing their authority. On the other hand, I have served on committees where the obligation to talk overwhelmed the necessity to act. A willful chairman may distort every proposal to his own advantage. The essential seems to be a dedication to the purposes for which a committee is formed rather than self-promotion by the members.

One of the fascinating irrelevancies of committee meetings lies in the doodles created by the members as they sit and listen to the proceedings. Many go in for elaborate geometric designs, which they build up endlessly. I used to construct little sentences written in hieroglyphic. I had to stop that when a neighbor asked if he might keep my doodle. I was embarrassed and refused rather rudely. I had written about the oratory of another member: "Wearisome is all this. Great-of-Mouth is the name of that man. His mouth speaks; his heart is silent." I could not risk the chance that my neighbor would ask for a translation.

There is a tendency to scorn committees as reducing matters to the lowest common denominator and as offering solutions that are needlessly complicated. One witticism says that a camel looks like an animal constructed by a committee. I do not love committees. It is tiresome to fly from Chicago to New York, sit at a table for two days trying to find a formula for agreement and action, then return to Chicago at midnight. Yet I respect committees as a proper working compromise between the administrator, who may achieve immediate results by ignoring the ideas of others, and the full legislative assembly, which does not have the time to learn all the complexities of a problem. A small and well-constructed committee can achieve results by close acquaintance of the members. The common bond of experience makes friends. I have good memories of these casual contacts. How otherwise could I have had the opportunity to sit at a table between the novelist Esther Forbes and the physicist Robert Oppenheimer?

TWELVE

COMMUNITY OF SCHOLARS

H E WHO deals with the ancient Orient has chosen a field apart
in place and time. By definition he is a separate individual. He
has entered an unusual field and has persisted in it against all
advice and in an uncertainty of employment. Often he is the
only scholar of his specialty at his institution. He has not arrived at distinction quickly. There has had to be a slow accumulation of lore and of mastery over his field before he could develop his own particular specialty and gain recognition. His
students may be few and far between. The nature of his career
has made him an Ishmael, roaming in deserts away from the
active centers. Cartoonists, with their passion to exaggerate, have
made the archaeologist or the Egyptologist a creature of monstrous eccentricity.

One of Breasted's hopes in founding the Oriental Institute was
to combat this isolation by bringing Orientalists together within
one building to provide them with a community where there
would be mutual stimulation of their genius. The academic staff

was chosen for distinction, and younger men of promise were added. They came from eight different countries. Outside of their profession they had few interests in common. Most of them were appointed because they had achieved some intellectual breakthrough in a difficult subject. They were individuals, and they persisted in being individuals. I have already said that we younger men joked about the feuding among our seniors and then ourselves voiced strong disagreement when we reached our own maturity. There were honest attempts to join scholars together in common projects of study and publication. Some of the field men did work handsomely in a team. They were the exception rather than the rule.

The most ambitious project that called for teamwork has been a dictionary of cuneiform, a vast historical compendium of the language usually called Assyrian. This kind of program promises to take at least a dozen years and is normally financed by a national or international agency. After forty years of Oriental Institute work, the dictionary is now appearing regularly, volume by volume. But it had its long period of stagnation. Before 1936, when money was available and jobs were scarce, there was an active staff in Chicago, scholars elsewhere were paid for contributions, and a vast accumulation of files was built up. After funds dwindled for the home staff and ceased for the foreign collaborators, the project slowed down to a crawl. Scholars gave their energies to personal research and offered the dictionary an abstracted left hand. There was a wealth of material, but no one was grinding out the articles to define the words.

In the 1950s sharp disagreement arose as to what a dictionary should be. A respectable school of thought argued that the Assyriological world was expecting firm answers to perplexing problems and wanted conclusive definitions of terms; before any defining article was completed, there should be mature consideration and full agreement by a committee of scholars. The opposing argument was that a dictionary was a working tool and not a solution to end all research. It was important to get it published, however imperfect, so that it might be improved through usage. Since each side was motivated by principle, the debate shifted from the practical to the moral. Three successive directors of the institute reviewed the arguments and decided in favor of prompt publication. A counsel of perfection would have delayed this massive project to the point where it would never appear.

Credit for the steady appearance of the *Assyrian Dictionary*, with a new volume appearing nearly every year, goes to the tireless devotion of Professor Leo Oppenheim. Few scholars would have been willing to dedicate their careers to a task which could be a dreary routine. Some scholarly reviews have praised the published volumes with faint damns. Yet everywhere there is acceptance and gratitude for the immense offering of material and the tentative conclusions drawn.

A few years ago an anonymous donor gave the University of Chicago a sum of money to establish the John A. Wilson Professorship in Oriental Studies. It is an immense pleasure to me that Professor Oppenheim is the first holder of that chair.

Scholarly feuds begin honestly as disagreements on matters of principle. What is the best way to reach a needed goal? As the disagreements proceed by further argument they become more pointed. When a high moral point is thrust at one's throat, some malice may be felt behind the thrust. Then it may become a personal feud animated by individual indignation. If one goes back and examines the arguments, one can always respect the honest logic that first prompted each debater.

The majority of scholars in the Oriental Institute comprises linguists dealing with ancient writings. That is the discipline they understand and respect most easily, and they feel most comfortable if the administrator is one of their own. When the right candidate for director of the institute or for chairman of the department is sought, debates, though always couched in parliamentary language, may become heated. If a non-linguist appears as a candidate, there may be vigorous political activity in the corridors. Oriental studies are not unique in forming pressure blocs for political purposes. One always hears tales about the maneuvering for power in other departments. There as here, if our Caesar seems ambitious, he has come to identify the good of Rome with his own good.

In their writings scholars may attack one another in more vigorous language than they would use in verbal debate. The language of academic disagreement is superficially polite. A colleague is not accused of lying, but it may be said that his "curious statement does not seem to be fully responsive to the facts." If he has appropriated some of my ideas without giving me credit, I may welcome him warmly to the point of view that I enunciated several months ago. If I believe that a colleague has been talking sheer nonsense, I may say, "We all recognize the imagination and enterprise which has brought forth this novel suggestion—if I may say so, this extremely novel suggestion." Academicians do not whack with a saber or pink with a foil. They try to draw visible blood by a slight stab with a rapier. It is a stylized performance at which some professors excel.

Yet we are not always so separatist. The *Assyrian Dictionary* remains a monument to collaboration. The field expeditions have normally been successful because of good teamwork. Henri Frankfort was able to summon unexpected resources from others. He drew some of us together in a series of lectures on ancient man's ideas about himself and his universe. In 1958 Carl Kraeling brought us all together for a conference on the beginnings of city life in the ancient Near East. Left to themselves, Orientalists nurture their own particular specialties. When presented with a real challenge by an attractive personality, they will work together for mutual stimulation. At the time of the Nubian emergency in the early 1960s Egyptologists and other scholars joined forces in trying to find the means to rescue monuments along the Nile.

On the international scene I have been aware of politics since I was a student. The French and the British were hostile to the

"German school" of Egyptology. Breasted, who had been a student under Adolf Erman in Berlin, leaned toward the Germans. The British conquerors of Egypt in the 1880s had left cultural matters, including archaeology, to the guidance of the French. An unbroken succession of Frenchmen served as directors-general of the Antiquities Service. The standards for good field work had been set by such Englishmen as Petrie and Griffith, and in this area were followed faithfully by the Germans and the Americans.

The tensions became clearer when I went to work in Egypt. There was a perceptible atmosphere of jealousy and rivalry. When Breasted offered the Egyptian Government the Rockefeller proposal for a new museum and training institute, the defeat of this overture sharply illustrated archaeological antagonisms. An admirable idea crashed on the irrational reefs of international and personal politics. Although Egyptian and Arab nationalism in the 1920s was political rather than cultural, the control of archaeology soon became a battleground for national ambition. A good antiquities law might be administered as an instrument against foreign excavators, but the basic motivation was that understandable emotion, self-determination, and such hostile possessiveness frustrated good field work.

Most of the excavation laws in the Near East promise the excavator a "representative share" of the things he finds. The digger hopes for a division at least fifty-fifty by value. However, the result may be conditioned by politics. When there is antiforeign feeling a government official may allot only a few minor pieces to the excavator as the "representative share." The foreign archaeologist then feels that his efforts have hardly been justified in terms of the antiquities he is allowed to take home. On the other hand, when the Egyptian Government wanted to encourage outside expeditions to work in Nubia, it promised a generous division and fulfilled that promise beyond expectations. Any law may be administered in radically different ways.

In 1935 the Italian Government sent a high official to the

International Congress of Orientalists in Rome, to assure the delegates that, while light may have come from the Orient in ancient times, it was now the duty of Western nations to return a newer light to the East. Cultural imperialism was being used to justify military imperialism, the Italian invasion of Ethiopia. Mussolini had governed Italy for many years by then, and Hitler had recently come to power in Germany. One could sense the peril threatening scholars in Central Europe as one saw individuals approach Breasted in the hope of finding positions in American universities. Yet I still had the naïve belief that proper work in fields as remote from the present day as Egyptology and Assyriology would not be damaged by politics. Only later would I see the decimation of the scholarly world in Germany and the war's destruction of promising young men in England. We still say wistfully that matters of culture should not be affected by politics. We must continue to act in that hope so that it may be partially true.

In 1947 a brave attempt was made to form a society for workers in our field. The first meeting of the International Association of Egyptologists was held in Copenhagen. The most respected authorities in the field were unable to attend, and there was visible jockeying for position by men who did not command the same following. The association has withered and died. The only admirable result has been the annual bibliography for Egyptology. However, that product owes more to the dedicated labors of some Dutch scholars than to the patronage of an association that has ceased to function. The Assyriologists are to be envied. They seem to have as many tensions and rifts as the Egyptologists, yet for several years they have been able to assemble for a scholarly conference. We need a vigorous initiative, a respected leader, and sufficient funds to maintain a secretariat for the formative years. Egyptology is well served by periodicals, but there is no substitute for personal acquaintance and personal conversation.

The sharpest antagonisms seem to be within nations rather than between nations. Paid positions in Egyptology are few, and there may be vicious competition for any one opening. One hears of sharper antagonisms among scholars of West Germany than between those of West and East Germany. After the Second World War there was a deep cleavage between two camps of French Egyptologists, based in part upon their loyalties during that struggle. In England it was alleged that some of the prize posts were awarded on the basis of whether a candidate was a gentleman or not. I am too close to the American scene to see similar tensions, unless it be a cleavage between the institutions of the Northeast and those of the West.

In 1960, in advance of the International Congress of Orientalists in Moscow, an American committee was formed and charged with the cordial mission of inviting the congress to come to the United States in 1963. The timing proved to be unfortunate. The trial of the American pilot whose U-2 plane had been shot down over the Soviet Union was going on at the time of the congress. No Russian could show any cordiality to any American. A Russian colleague with whom I had had very pleasant relations in Cairo could only shake my hand, say a few formal words, and then turn away in embarrassment. There was none of that relaxed sociability that had lightened the previous congress in Munich. We were treated with cold civility, allowed to present our papers, taken on the sightseeing tours that had been advertised in advance, and then ignored. The atmosphere, like the weather, was dark and cool. At the same time the Russians were suffering. Hundreds of delegates from Communist China who had been expected were withdrawn in a last-minute boycott of the Soviet Union. The Russians learned how the program of a convention may be damaged by defections just before the meeting.

Only our leading delegate, Norman Brown, was privy to the maneuvers within the Russian-constructed steering committee.

The Americans were prepared to offer an invitation for the next congress. Our hosts tried desperately to find a substitute invitation, so that the Americans could be turned down. They allegedly persuaded an Egyptian to wire his government, seeking a bid from a country acceptable to the Soviet Union. While he was doing this, the delegates from India decided they could offer an invitation resting upon their neutrality. The Russians promptly dropped their Egyptian colleague and pushed through acceptance of the Indian proposal. At least that is what rumor told us. In 1964 at New Delhi the Americans were able to present their invitation successfully.

After the congress in Moscow, Mary and I joined the party that visited Tashkent, Samarkand, and Bokhara in Asiatic Russia. The Asiatic Russians had none of that glum intensity that had made our stay in Moscow so somber. They were ready to talk and laugh with us, even to play jokes on us. A girl approached an American professor and held out a small book and a pen. He was honored that she seemed to want his autograph and signed with a flourish. She immediately whipped out a red kerchief and knotted it around his neck. She had enrolled him in the Young Pioneers! Our party of forty Orientalists was too much for Samarkand, where the hotel ran out of food after two meals, and for Tashkent, where the water failed in the bathrooms. But the sights were splendid and the company good.

We were also too much for the Intourist Agency, which had arranged and was guiding our tour. They wanted us to see silk factories and collective farms. We wanted to see mosques, churches, and synagogues. There was a running argument between the scholarly tourists and the guides. Finally, at the end of our stay, they relented, and there was a mosque service in Tashkent for our benefit. Old men in brilliant robes were almost weeping with joy at being allowed to worship publicly. They responded eagerly to our few words of Arabic. To my distress we were encouraged to walk among them and to photograph them as they prayed. The aggressive young mufti who made a speech of welcome was a distinct contrast to the shy old worshipers. At least we had had our way, even if the service seemed to be staged and thus not typical of religion in the Soviet Union.

After we had returned to Moscow I met the young Intourist guide who had been so harassed by our demands. He invited me to join him in a toast to "peace and friendship," which I was happy to do. Then he asked me about what had been troubling him. "Mr. Wilson, are all Western scholars so independent-minded?" I gave the question due consideration and then solemnly assured him that, yes, all Western scholars were indeed very independent-minded. He seemed to feel that this was distressingly undisciplined.

In preparation for the congress I had spent evenings studying Russian. I listened to records and wrote out exercises in Cyrillic script. My chief stumbling block was the inflection of the verbs, so that I settled down to a single tense and mood. Thus equipped, I felt able to ask directions in the street or to order breakfast in our hotel room. Although we always ordered the same meal, it came to us in perplexing variety. This was probably due to my inadequate command of the language, but I excused myself by claiming that the maid brought us whatever was available in the kitchen.

Mary and I explored the city on foot. We discovered a bookshop that carried paperbacks in English. The prize was a little booklet of Chinese folktales rendered into English. One tale was about a wise fool named something like Hoca Li. He played tricks on his rural neighbors, just as Nasreddin Hoja of the Near East (the Egyptian Goha) had done. He borrowed a pot from another villager, and when he returned it he brought back a tiny pot with it. When asked about this, he explained that the first pot had had a baby. This occurred a second time, and then the neighbors whispered to each other how silly Hoca was. So a friend willingly loaned him a huge cooking pot. Hoca failed to return this. The neighbor finally demanded it. "Oh," said Hoca, "didn't I tell you? I'm sorry, but your pot died!" To have found the same story all the way across Asia was a delight.

On a Sunday we took the Moscow subway and visited the zoo,

which was crowded with mothers and fathers and children. They were all having so happy a family time that some of them were smiling, even though they were Muscovites. On another day I went to the American Embassy for mail, without my passport, which was held at the hotel desk. Two burly policemen closed in on me and questioned me. I made the mistake of trying to answer in Russian, which only compounded their suspicions. After the second exchange of question and answer, my command of the language failed. At last I discovered in my pocket the invitation to the congress written in Russian and in English. This identified me, and they let me pass. A little knowledge is so dangerous a thing that it should be concealed in pretended ignorance. Moscow was always interesting, but the air seemed very free in Copenhagen when our plane took us there after the congress.

In 1967 The International Congress of Orientalists was to come to the United States, to the campus of the University of Michigan. We had a planning committee composed impartially of representatives from the American Oriental Society and the Association for Asian Studies. The attitudes of the classicists, who normally dealt with ancient languages, and of the modernists, who leaned toward the social sciences, were both represented. The modernists wanted a program cemented with theme and purpose. They argued that the sessions would profit by the selection of problems common to the whole Orient instead of problems limited to a single culture. There should be panels, to which the best authorities would be invited to contribute their accumulated wisdom. We could then discuss education, population trends, development economics, or the interplay of modern law with traditional law. Instead of an afternoon session given over to seven unrelated papers by seven different scholars, the gathering could focus interest upon one common theme.

That made sense on the face of it. But I had to consider the traditionalists in the field. I could not let a classicist give up his

right to talk about his own dear little subject. For someone concerned with agriculture in modern Turkey the "structured program" would be attractive. But the man who had made a discovery about a verbal usage in a Phoenician inscription would
want to talk about that. If he had his personal paper to offer, he
might convince his university to pay his travel expenses, but not
if he came only as an auditor. I had to defend the right of my
individualists to continue their time-hallowed practices. The
social scientists accepted the fact that you cannot "structure"
some people.

The program was fixed, with individual papers in regional
sections in the mornings and panel discussions covering the
whole Orient in the afternoons. The schedule was in print. All
the difficult negotiations to raise money for the congress had
gone as far as they could. The charter flights from Paris and
Tokyo had been filled, and the secretariat at Ann Arbor was
dealing with last-minute appeals. Professor A from Europe
thought that the wealthy Americans could finance his trip more
generously than they had offered. Professor B insisted that his
wife must be brought into the charter flight at the same discount
rate he had been granted. Professor C was slow in sending in his
registration forms. He then discovered that a student of his had
been accepted for one of the charter flights, whereas he had
been placed on a waiting list. He threatened to punish that student unless this gross injustice were remedied. American scholars
were aggrieved that foreigners were receiving subventions toward their travel, whereas they, representatives of a host country
that was trying to put on a brilliant display of scholarship, were
receiving nothing. Trying to organize and run an international
congress is like being pecked to death by geese.

Then, just as the deadline approached and the books had been
closed, just days before the congress was to open, there came a
request from the Soviet Union to postpone the congress indefinitely because of the tense international situation. In that summer
of 1967 the international situation was no more tense than usual.

The six-day war between Israel and the Arab states was over. There was no electric threat in the air a few weeks after that struggle. Scholars could travel freely from one country to another. It was true that Detroit had been shaken by racial violence in recent months, but that did not affect Ann Arbor. What was this new tension? Apparently the Russians were engaged in a ploy to throw the Americans off balance, as they themselves had been thrown off balance by the defection of the Chinese seven years earlier. The answer went back to them that it was too late to change the date and the actuality of the congress. The Soviet Union withdrew permission for any of its scholars to attend the meeting and put pressure upon the satellites to do the same.

The table had been set, the place cards had been carefully distributed, and the soup was simmering on the back of the stove. We were all prepared for a feast of academic learning. For my sections on the ancient Near East I had one hundred and sixty-eight papers on the program, with another dozen in reserve if time permitted. Now more than twenty-five papers had been withdrawn. We were sure only about those from the Soviet Union; it was not clear what satellites might ignore the ban against appearing. Added to this was the normal attrition of scholars who at the last minute were unable to come. The congress became a shambles. The printed program was a mockery. The section chairmen for the different regional or functional sessions had to do a desperate scissors-and-paste job every day. Papers that had been placed on the waiting list could now be inserted into the program—if the waiting scholar could be located and notified that he was to read his offering at such-and-such a time in such-and-such a room.

There were cries of dismay around the campus; there was the usual confusion at a mammoth conference about who was meeting where and when. Yet the congress took place. In view of the last-minute withdrawals one might almost say that it was a success. The subsection on Caucasian studies heard three of the proposed six papers; that on Central Asian studies one out of three. Egyptology was more fortunate; no papers were listed from any of the defecting countries. We not only had a good program; we also had a pleasant time socially. The Assyriologists took time after the congress to visit the University of Chicago and held one of their periodic conferences.

After the hurly-burly at Ann Arbor, it was a relaxed pleasure to attend the next congress at Canberra, Australia, in January 1971. My only responsibilities were to read a paper and serve as a delegate from the American Oriental Society. Only seventeen papers were listed for the ancient Near East, as against one hundred and sixty-eight at Ann Arbor. Even though it was during the heat of the Australian summer there was no tension, political or otherwise. One could shed jacket and tie, attend the morning sessions, take a long siesta in the afternoon or go off to the animal sanctuary to look at the emus and kangaroos.

THIRTEEN

SPEAKING AND WRITING

An autobiography is like a road across the open prairies, where the landscape is featured by a string of telephone poles—I . . . I . . . I . . . I . . . I. To some degree the author's "I's" give an account of the traffic he has seen passing along the road. To some degree he may report the messages he personally has transmitted along the way. Like Tennyson's Ulysses, he has become a part of all that he has seen. My ideas of yesterday have been cast off on the basis of experience. My public speeches and my writings reflect changes within Egyptology over half a century.

Speakers are made, not born. They must learn by painful experience. Unlike Demosthenes, I did not put pebbles into my mouth to achieve better articulation. Figuratively I had to pull out the pebbles that were naturally there. Once, when I was a graduate student, I wanted to show my erudition at a learned meeting by commenting on a paper read by somebody else. In my first sentence I tried to say, "We Egyptologists have been so concerned with pharaonic ceremonies that we have neglected the simpler aspects of religion." This came out, "We Egyptologists have been so concerned with pharaonic cemeteries that we have neglected. . . ." I took a deep breath, went back, and started over again. Once more "pharaonic ceremonies" came out "pharaonic cemeteries." On the third attempt I did succeed in saying the phrase correctly, finished that sentence, but was too confused to develop my point. I sat down hastily. The lesson was never to try a word like "pharaonic" again.

Learning has come slowly and painfully. One side of me has demanded the exact word, that professional term which means precisely one thing. The other side of me has warned that an audience might be lost if they have to grapple with such jargon as "pharaonic ceremonies," "synchronistic dynasties," or "the law of frontality." A speaker has to meet his audience at least halfway. The right speech must not be made to the wrong audience. A class of twelve-year-olds or a Rotary Club is not the same as the American Oriental Society. Also, the same speech should never be given a second time in exactly the same way. As with my classes, I have had to find some way of igniting a fresh spark of excitement in myself if I expected to ignite interest in others. In 1960–61, when I gave essentially the same talk about saving the Nubian monuments eighty times within fifteen months, I struggled desperately to introduce a different illustration or incident, so that it would not be droned out as if recorded on tape. The challenge of a speech has not been dulled by long experience. I am always tense and abstracted ahead of time, mentally revising the essential points. How a lecturer can digest a dinner before his evening speech is an unsolved mystery to me.

In the course of time I was accepted as an orator, in demand for memorial services or presentation ceremonies. I should like to reject the words "orator" and "lecturer" and accept the word "speaker." But often the demand rested on that dictionary definition of an "oration: an elaborate or dignified discourse, esp. one delivered on some special occasion, as a funeral or an anniversary." I was called upon to function at the annual meeting of a society of obstetricians and gynecologists or at an event honoring somebody's seventieth birthday. When President Truman was unable to leave the White House to address the annual meeting of the American Library Association, I was alerted to pinch-hit for him. The members of the association had not known who the speaker would be and so were not disappointed to get an ancient Egyptian underworld instead of Harry Truman's particular type of hell.

On two successive years a bankers' summer school at the University of Wisconsin was let down by announced speakers. On each occasion a telephone summons came to me in Chicago in the morning, so that I was able to fly to Madison for an afternoon talk. The second time the withdrawing speaker was Senator Barry Goldwater. That gave me a sure-fire opening line. I had been introduced as a specialist on ancient Egypt. I told the bankers that their program chairman had originally planned to give them a speaker who would take them back two hundred years. In his place I was able to compound the interest by taking them back three thousand years.

My worst experience came on a wintry morning when I was called out of class by an urgent telephone call from an officer of the university. It appeared that it was Ladies' Day at the Chicago Executives Club. Fifteen hundred persons would assemble in the ballroom of a downtown hotel in about forty-five minutes. But the scheduled speaker, Jerry Lewis, was snowed in at the New York airport and could not reach Chicago in time for the luncheon. Would I go downtown and talk to them off the cuff? My mind began calculating a timetable: so many minutes to dismiss class, go home, change clothes, and travel downtown. It was possible, and it would be a service to the university. I agreed, and I asked to have a taxi pick me up immediately. Only after I had hung up and was hurrying back to the classroom did the full message penetrate my mind. Jerry Lewis? Jerry Lewis, the comedian! What had I let myself in for? It was a disappointed audience, but I was grateful that they listened patiently to my account of the problems of modern Egypt.

Then, as on other occasions, my talk was about the modern

Near East, with a sympathetic presentation of the Arab side. I have made many such talks over the past twenty years, and I have learned from bitter experience not to join in a panel discussion about the Arab-Israeli conflict. Such "discussions" are almost always displays of unreasoning bad temper, often ending in a shouting match. Since I can usually see some reason for the opposing attitude, I have always been at a disadvantage in such a debate. It is too bad that international relations are governed by emotion rather than reason.

On my seventieth birthday colleagues and former students surprised me by presenting me with a volume of essays written for the occasion. I was speechless.

Writing a speech and writing a book have very different motivations and circumstances. A speech may be revised as it goes on: a book is a single occasion, produced for an indefinite future. The book is final. The invitation to give a speech may be declined. When one has a book inside one's system, the agonizing period of gestation must go on until "the baby" is delivered.

I wrote one book during a steaming Chicago summer in an unsheathed attic room, where the temperature must have exceeded 105 degrees at times. This hideaway was too remote for me to hear the telephone or the doorbell. The paper stuck to my perspiring hands, but my only concern was to write clearly and accurately. Write, read, rewrite, reread, discard, rewrite, revise. I have never had a research assistant to gather material or to do the preliminary writing. This has to be mine, down to forming the index. The result is never satisfactory in a final sense, but since the book must be produced, one has finally to stop. Writing is hard work, but the author has the same proud and defensive love for the book that a mother has for her baby.

That love may not appear in the names I have inflicted upon my brain children. *The Burden of Egypt*, subtitled *An Interpretation of Ancient Egyptian Culture* (1951), was a title chosen from the Book of Isaiah. It tried to express my belief that Egypt's brilliant rise was followed by a long fall. There were triumph and tragedy in the story, as distinct from the triumph only, which earlier writers had emphasized. But who now responds to the fine cadences of the King James version of the Bible and remembers the successive "burdens"? Daily Bible readings in our home had etched that phrase in my memory. It might not catch the interest of a browser in a bookstore. When the University of Chicago Press put it into paperback and changed the title to *The Culture of Ancient Egypt* (1956), it became a steady sales item, running through eleven impressions thus far.

In *The Burden* the Introduction starts with the sentence: "This is not a history of ancient Egypt, but rather a book about ancient Egyptian history." I then go on to explain that my purpose is less to establish chains of facts than to try to find out what the most important facts mean. Most people have ignored that statement and have treated the book as a history. According to one reviewer, it is cultural history, but "far too subjective and over-burdened with speculation." That is precisely what I intended. The historian has two tasks, the first to assemble the facts and the second to puzzle about the material, spiritual, and psychological motivations behind the facts. It is the latter that interests me and that accounts for my subjectivity.

This book has one prize sentence that has not been rooted out even after its ambiguity was detected. There is a chronological table with the dates for the dynasties and the names of the more important kings. Above this listing of names and dates stands the sentence: "Names not in this book have been omitted."

The Book of Nehemiah supplied the title for the record of American archaeological work in Egypt, *Signs and Wonders upon Pharaoh* (1964). A reader might have preferred the subtitle, *A History of American Egyptology*, but that seemed to me dull and pretentious. The present reader may be glad that I resisted the temptation of going to the Book of Exodus for this volume and naming it "We Sat by the Fleshpots of Egypt." Every writer of history must remember that his works will be dated and will have only a limited currency. I have tried to tell my students that what I tell them is always subject to change, that they will be privileged to revise written history by their own discoveries and interpretations.

Of all the writings I take the most pride in my chapters in the volume that resulted from the series of lectures on the ideas of ancient man, mentioned earlier. Written jointly by H. and H. A. Frankfort, John A. Wilson, Thorkild Jacobsen, and William A. Irwin, the book was titled *The Intellectual Adventure of Ancient Man*, and subtitled *An Essay on Speculative Thought in the Ancient Near East* (1946); later, in paperback, it was abridged and called *Before Philosophy* (1949). Jacobsen's part in those lectures was the most profound and revolutionary, bringing the Sumerians into clarity for the first time. My own contribution was subjective and tentative. Nevertheless I had the feeling that I had come closer to understanding the ancient Egyptian mind than in any other attempt I have made. I had just returned from the war years in Washington and found that I could look at my field afresh. Frankfort's original analysis of ancient psychology ignited us all, and we were emboldened to try to understand more clearly. My chapters were overloaded with technical words and difficult concepts, but I was trying to climb into the minds of the ancients to see how they thought. Such speculation either hit the bull's eye or missed the target completely.

The emphases in *The Intellectual Adventure* and *The Burden of Egypt* offer some idea of how I have been affected by current Egyptological thought and of how I have deviated from such thought.

The unusual attention given to the geography of Egypt as an influence upon the character of the people I consider justified, in the sense that one then starts out with factors that are physical and cannot be denied, but this should not overshadow other factors that are present but not so visible. The geographic separateness of Egypt gave its people a sense of security and a sense of being The People, superior to all their immediate neighbors. The physical balance of the Nile cliffs and the interplay of Nile and desert offered a strong feeling of geometric solidity, on which were built the tolerance for opposing forces. The warming sun and the periodicity of the Nile inundation induced some laxity, and also gave a strong love of life and an optimism about life after death. This emphasis was my own.

Frankfort's "multiplicity of approach" I accepted wholeheartedly—that is, the argument that the ancients did not select one explanation of a phenomenon but believed that a world of divine miracle was capable of different causations. For example, the different myths about the creation were all instances of the productive purposes of the gods and thus reassured man that the gods worked in different ways to achieve the same goals. What may seem to us moderns as irreconcilable they took as complementary and thus as confirming the manifold powers of the gods. Although the ancient logic is not our logic, it had its own consistency and integrity. One has to leave the world of rational scientific causality and enter the world of expected miracles to understand this.

Distinctly my own was the doctrine that all phenomena of the universe were regarded by the Egyptians as parts of the same general substance. There was no dividing line between man and god, between man and animal, between god and plant, and so on. The universe was described as a spectrum in which one color could become another under changing conditions. A god might be unseen in the atmosphere or take visible form in the sun disk, in a statue, in an animal, in a plant, in a mountain, or in a city. The Egyptians did not pigeonhole the elements in their universe but believed that these flowed freely from one form to another. "Consubstantiality" still seems basic to the understanding of the ancient mind, although I should now prefer a different bit of jargon, "protean capacity." One has to admit exceptions, partial or whole, to this doctrine.

One such exception is the dogma that the king of Egypt was a god, and his rule was accepted in diverse parts of the land because he came from the realm of the gods and not from one province or city. Therefore he ruled because he was different. This idea was certainly not new even then, but it had to be reconciled with the earlier theory that there was no substantive difference among the phenomena of the universe. That was made possible by the principle of free substitution, that he who had seemed to be a man might become recognized as a king, therefore as a god. When there was change from one dynasty to another, religion would assert that this being who had served as a provincial noble had in fact been procreated by the sun god and might thus be accepted as divine.

To define what is a god or a half-god or a spiritual intercessor between man and god is difficult. I fall back on the spectrum, where red is different from yellow but there is no sharp sectioning, so that it is possible to pass from red through orange to yellow without leaving the system. Ancient Egyptian tolerance tried to keep all forces in some kind of balance, and an easy way to do so was to blur differences.

In the controversy set in motion by Alexander Scharff in *Zeitschrift für ägyptische Sprache* (1935) and by Henri Frankfort in *The American Journal of Semitic Languages and Literatures* (1941), I was on their side. They listed artistic and architectural phenomena in early Mesopotamia and early Egypt that seemed to indicate a Babylonian priority. This became for me the "Mesopotamian stimulation" that rapidly changed predynastic Egypt from prehistory into history, from rusticity into civilization, from illiteracy into writing. The evidence cited seemed indisputable, and I embraced their theory openly, though reluctantly. My lack of enthusiasm was a legacy from Breasted, who loved Egypt so much that he saw its culture as independently creative and not influenced from the outside. Many of the factors that contributed to this theory have stood up over the past thirty years, but the mechanism of such an alleged

Mesopotamian influence upon the Nile Valley has become doubtful. Many of the phenomena appear in Nubia, Upper Egypt, and the deserts, where such a cultural priority would have been least likely to penetrate. There must be continued debate on the matter. For me the argument will have little relation to the old dispute as to whether Egypt or Mesopotamia was the "cradle of civilization." You may choose your separate factors and use them to define "civilization" and thus argue for the priority of either culture. In certain respects Babylonia seems to have led; in others, Egypt.

Another thesis in my writings has been that the best of ancient Egypt came in the first five dynasties and that thereafter the culture was no longer creative; it became repetitive and never again showed the same inventive brilliance as at the beginning. Again the terms may be defined to fit the argument. What is "first," "new," or "best"? It is difficult for an American to accept a psychology that was retrospective rather than progressive. In defining what was best or what was characteristically Egyptian I set up my own standards. The basic illustration of early achievement was the amazing architecture of the Great Pyramid, never matched in the later dynasties, indeed never surpassed in other cultures. Egyptian architectural mastery went downhill from that point, and a similar decline in other techniques and attitudes could be argued. Other scholars have used different factors for the same argument.

From the premise that the Old Kingdom was the model age for later Egypt, it followed that the Egyptians of that period set the standard for men of following ages. Their art and their literature agree. They seemed to be positive, without great depth. They were full of spunk and vinegar, humorous, sly, quick to anger but immediately forgiving, pragmatic in accepting whatever worked, and full of bouncing optimism. If they were by no means a majestic people, they were very likable. Their cheery confidence went over into their view of death, which they denied as a finality. They relished this world so dearly that they extended it into the next world and asserted that their paradise would be like the Nile Valley in its richest aspects. I find this debatable. Whereas one scholar may insist that the Egyptians did not fear death but welcomed it as a rich extension of life, another may feel that they seemed to protest too much, that they dreaded death so fearfully that they tried to deny its existence. The truth might be compounded out of both viewpoints. We all have a love-fear attitude toward the great transitions of existence, and we may stress only the love element and try to suppress the fear.

I accepted Breasted's claim, last stated in *The Dawn of Conscience* (1933), that the period between the Old and Middle Kingdoms showed the blossoming of a social conscience, with a genuine care for poor people and an approach toward equalitarianism. However, I felt that this was a product of hard times in Egypt and that when prosperity returned in the Middle Kingdom the attempt to find social justice was abandoned. Ancient Egypt deserves all praise for asserting that the poor man had the same rights as the great man, but also reproof that she did not hang on to that concept and make it real. It has to be said that all our arguments are based on what the upper classes wrote in antiquity. The lower classes were inarticulate, except insofar as the establishment claimed to speak for them. We baste together our elaborate patchwork of theories using only the swatches of cloth that are at hand. If other pieces had survived our pattern might be very different.

Even though I have denied that the First Intermediate Period, between the Old and Middle Kingdoms, had made any lasting change in Egyptian character, I have placed a reverse emphasis on the Second Intermediate Period, when Egypt was ruled by foreign conquerors. The psychology of the time was rather dramatically called "the Great Humiliation." It has been argued that the shock of domination by outsiders ended Egyptian complacency and security. Egypt felt obliged to go out and conquer the world, both for her own safety and to re-establish her sense of superiority. The resultant empire dominated all the territory that could be reached by foot soldiers. Egypt became rich, international, and assertive. Architecture continued to be massive in order to seek eternity, but slow and solid workmanship was replaced by sheer mass, erected quickly without the feeling of everlasting repose. The culture became more interested in the present, at the cost of the eternal future. Then Egypt changed. To the subjective eye she was no longer the same organism. One might concentrate on this change and say that the culture was now intrinsically different; or one could stand off, view it as a whole, and insist that the more it changed the more it was the same. Certainly Egypt went on claiming that it was eternally unchanged, but for me imperialism reversed some of the factors that had been Egyptian.

My argument is that Egypt had been tolerant and accommodating, so that discord could be resolved by compromise, but the empire brought that one "irresponsible conflict," when the heretic pharaoh Akh-en-Aton seemed to reject all that was Egyptian. In point of fact it could be claimed that he tried to take a position that had been Egyptian in older times by forcing a return to the sole and central power of the pharaoh. He swept away the competing gods who had come to dominate the nation and substituted the life-giving power of the sun disk, which had no politics. For once, the system was not flexible enough, and tolerance broke down, because the other powers in the land had invested too much in the new Egypt to accept such a deviation from the existing forms. Akh-en-Aton's reforms were swept away, and the traditional forces returned in full power, seeking their justification in a religion that had itself been changed by empire. Though it may be true that a heretic was in part trying to re-establish an old orthodoxy, the period is too full of complexities and contradictions for this theory to be accepted without reservation. Egyptologists have their fiercest battles over the character and influence of Akh-en-Aton. Again I have parted from the teachings of Breasted in not admiring this pharaoh as much as he did. Akh-en-Aton's ideals may have been glorious, but his inflexibility was disastrous. He did not succeed in finding any accommodation of his fresh vision with the system. If his approach to monotheism had almost no understanding or acceptance within his own country, it cannot have affected other cultures. He becomes a figure out of Greek tragedy, right in his purposes yet pursued by the Furies.

My books drop Egypt rather abruptly about 1100 B.C., though she still had more than a thousand years of effective life, because I feel that the changes that came in under imperialism reversed the Egyptian system. The old easygoing tolerance and optimism were replaced by a disciplined obedience to mere form. The next world was no longer considered a joyous extension of this life, but only a dim justification for patience here. Although there were flashes of the old spirit, the millennium before the Romans took over was sterile and resigned. Texts went on repeating the old formulas of abundant life, but the spirit was dead. Obviously my argument is extreme. No system can last a thousand years unless it has some vital sap in it. Other scholars have pointed out genuine triumphs in later ages. I may have presented a partial truth as though it were the whole truth.

Not all of these ideas were mine, of course. Few of them would gain cordial acceptance by the entire Egyptological fraternity. I have been illustrating the slow ferment of ideas in our field. Some of what we may have embraced in the 1920s has been cast away. In our age of doubt and pessimism no one can present the history of Egypt with Breasted's infectious joy. So similarly what we now see as truth may appear to be absurd a generation from now.

I have tried to be balanced and tentative in my books. Others may be even more aware of my indecisiveness. In 1971, when our Nubian committee was discussing a problem in the restoration of a temple, the chairman summed up the argument by saying, "Well, gentlemen, it seems that, on the basis of the evidence, we can come to no firm conclusion."A young Egyptian inspector present was carrying the Arabic translation of my book. He held it up, grinned, and said, "It is just like *The Burden of Egypt!*"

The book about American archaeology in Egypt, *Signs and Wonders upon Pharaoh* (1964), was a pleasure to write because it was anecdotal, and I enjoy that form of communication. About 1960 it suddenly occurred to me that most of my students had been born since the death of Breasted and had no conception of what sort of a man he had been. Men whom I had known —Flinders Petrie, Howard Carter, George Reisner, Kurt Sethe —were names in books and not real persons to them. I began to remember a past that was just yesterday to me. Soon I found myself anxious to do another book. It could have been enlarged into a history of Oriental studies, but I did not feel competent to give a first-hand report on other fields and other cultures, and I wanted that personal authority to be visible. This may have made the book too restricted to merit great sales, which is disappointing, but I have never thought of money in connection with writing. If a book insists that it must be written, I obey.

In addition to my writings, I became involved in translating. When James B. Pritchard was editing the volume prepared by eleven contributors, *Ancient Near Eastern Texts relating to the Old Testament* (1950), I was asked if I would contribute translations of Egyptian inscriptions. I accepted without asking enough questions. It was much later that I found that the Asryrian, Sumerian, and Hittite texts had been divided among nine American scholars. Apparently it had been assumed that I would do some of the Egyptian texts and nominate other Egyptologists to do the rest. No one had the courage to stop me when I took on the whole job. The actual work took only about a year. It was based upon the files of translations that I had been building up for more than twenty years. My renderings were generally reliable, careful rather than literary, and unmarked by any flashes of genius. Indeed Sir Alan Gardiner, in the *Journal of Egyptian Archaeology* (1953), once showed that I had translated the lines in one broken text backward!

Some of my brain children have traveled abroad. *The Burden* has appeared in Arabic, Spanish, French, Italian, and, in modified form, in German. *The Intellectual Adventure* has come out in German, Spanish, Hebrew, and Serbian. As I look at some of these translations I realize that it is a wise father who knows his own child.

FOURTEEN

꩜꩜꩜꩜꩜꩜

NUBIAN RESCUE

THE Nile Valley, as seen from the air, is a tawny and gray desert, lonely, forbidding, yet strangely beautiful. Across this wilderness cuts the broad brown stream of the river, feeding a band of vivid green on each shore. The eternal battle between life and death leaps forcefully to one's eyes.

The mechanics of the Nile seem to have the air of a planned ingenuity—I mean the movement of the Nile before man added his ingenuities of dams and canals. The lakes far south on the equator feed the White or "Clear" Nile, which proceeds northward into the Sudan at a leisurely pace. There its slow course used to be impeded even more by floating islands of vegetation, the Sudd. Much of the silt has been deposited before this stream reaches Khartum, which is why it is relatively "clear." At Khartum it is joined by its more turbulent partner, the Blue or "Dark" Nile, rushing down impetuously from Ethiopia after the summer rains. Before man slowed it down by dams, it was this more urgent Blue Nile that caused the annual inundation, which used to reach a peak in Egypt early in September. At Khartum the vigorous push of the Blue Nile holds back the more placid waters of the White Nile, so that the latter stream may continue to water Egypt after the inundation has dashed through the land. I wished that it had been feasible to have a scale model of these hydrodynamics to show my classes.

The annual flood used to stretch out over the Egyptian fields, resting for a few weeks and depositing a thin film of fertilizing silt. Then it would flush back into the bed of the river, and men would begin their crops. By spring the Nile would be a low, sluggish stream. To hold the flood as long as possible, ancient man caught the water in earthen basins. In the Delta a system of canals were used to carry water out to the spreading fields, but canals were used only sparingly in Middle Egypt and not at all in Upper Egypt. The difference between mean high and mean low Nile used to be twenty feet at the First Cataract, sixteen at Cairo. A markedly low Nile meant famine. A markedly high Nile would wash away the dikes and melt the mud-brick villages. Since Greek times men have repeated the truism that Egypt is the gift of the Nile. With the Egyptians one can come to love and fear the river.

Only land that could be irrigated from the Nile could grow the crops to feed the people. That little strip of soil was densely crowded in antiquity. Population dropped off under weak governments, increased under stable governments. When Napoleon invaded Egypt in 1798 the population was estimated to be between two and two and a half millions. In the census of 1897 the figure was close to ten million. To maintain such numbers better conservation of the water was necessary. It was proposed at that time to build a 130-foot-high dam south of Asswan at the First Cataract. There was a cry of protest from archaeologists. Many of the temples of Nubia, that stretch of shore between the First and Second Cataracts, would be affected by higher water. In particular the temples on the Island of Philae, "the pearl of Egypt," would be flooded for much of the year. Ominous predictions were made that these fine structures would be destroyed. But the dam was completed in 1903. Two later reconstructions raised its height by another thirty-five feet. Tourists during the winter season could see only the top of the pylon of the temple of Isis at Philae. The pavement of the temple was nearly sixty feet down in the water.

Modern health measures have permitted the population of Egypt to increase at a staggering rate. When the revolutionary government took over in 1952 the number of Egyptians was moving from twenty-five toward thirty million. The government decided upon a major operation, a new High Dam south of the First Cataract. This would back up a lake 300 miles long, impound water to be used twelve months of the year instead of seven, and give the land much more hydroelectric power. As in the case of the little dam sixty years earlier, this would obviously benefit the living Egyptians. But the vastly increased height over the previous level—180 more feet—would flood more than twenty Nubian temples and cover permanently 300 miles of little-known archaeological land. Should we then recognize the priority of the living, shrug our shoulders, and say, "Let the dead bury their dead"? In the earlier case we had merely regretted the loss of Philae; should we now turn to other matters?

There was a vigorous "No!" to these questions from several Egyptologists. More than one person faced up to this formidable challenge, but no one more resolutely than a French scholar, Mme. Christiane Desroches-Noblecourt. Her voice was insistent and undaunted by difficulties. Without her demand that Nubia must be saved before the High Dam was completed, some of the rest of us might not have bestirred ourselves. Further, there was now an agency that had not existed in 1900, the United Nations Educational, Scientific, and Cultural Organization, UNESCO for short. Mme. Noblecourt in Paris could be heard clearly at the UNESCO headquarters on the Place de Fontenoy. A salvage operation more massive than anything that had been known before would cost a staggering amount, and UNESCO was notoriously poor in the face of the many demands made upon it. Yet it was obviously this world force that should be concerned about this cultural problem.

Several small forays into the doomed land showed the dimensions of the problem. In June 1959 the executive board of UNESCO authorized a survey by specialists, who were to recommend what, if anything, could be done by an international effort. A commission of experts visited Nubia in the heat of October, headed by Dr. J. O. Brew of Harvard, who had been vigorous in pushing the investigation of American sites that had been threatened with flooding. The other American member of the commission was the late William C. Hayes of the Metropolitan Museum of Art in New York. We could have had no better representative.

The commission had a rugged trip, trying to see and judge everything in Egyptian Nubia. I remember a motion picture showing the Dutch member of the team picking a glutinous way through thick mud on a visit to a waterlogged temple. As he pulled each foot out of the slime a streamer of black muck clung trailingly to his sole. The weather was steaming, and most of the members were new to the area and to the problems. The commission grossly underestimated the cost, and concentrated more on saving temples than on the excavation needed. But a positive report was submitted, ending with the recommendation that the director-general of UNESCO make an international appeal to rescue "the Nubian historical, archaeological, and artistic heritage which forms part of the human cultural patrimony."

The United Arab Republic (Egypt) clearly expressed the sincerity of its request to UNESCO by reversing its former nationalistic attitude, which had jealously protected antiquities from foreign exploitation. President Nasser released a statement in which he said that the High Dam would be for the benefit of the people of Egypt, but the treasures from the ancient past were part of the heritage of all mankind. The U.A.R. was prepared to give excavators, in Egyptian Nubia at least, half of their finds, instead of that minimal representation that had been so common. Those institutions which worked in Nubia would later have priority for excavation in Egypt proper, and would be granted that more generous division of finds. Further, five Nubian temples and sundry other antiquities might be ceded to those countries which participated in the salvage work in a big way. Never before had such generous terms been offered to the excavator. In practice over the following years Egypt has faithfully carried out these liberal promises.

Early in March 1960 the director-general of UNESCO, Vittorino Veronese, launched an appeal to the nations of the world to save the Nubian antiquities. Later that month a group of Egyptologists, archaeologists, anthropologists, and museum curators met at the National Gallery in Washington to consider what the United States might do. It was expected that the Egyptologists would provide the ideas and the enthusiasm for an energetic campaign. This promised to be the biggest cultural cooperation ever undertaken and a pilot project for similar crises in other countries. Ill health and prior commitments kept two leading Egyptologists from the meeting. The others were unfortunately divided in their opinions. Perhaps we who deal with matters four thousand years old are not prepared to meet a deadline of five years. Certainly we were all absorbed in research projects of our own, which would engross our attention over the next year or two. None of us had ever excavated in Nubia, which presented archaeological problems different from those in Egypt itself. None of us expected our institutions to change existing budgets and provide large sums of money for such an emergency. One Egyptologist argued that Nubia was a poverty-stricken land in contrast to rich Egypt and that the bulk of the problem was the rescue of vast stone temples, which was a job for engineers rather than philologists. All of this had some truth, and the objections blunted the drive for a common effort. A few of us believed that if we evaded this challenge we should not be true to the cultural heritage from ancient Egypt that had been entrusted to us for study. This *was* our problem.

However, no one opposed the formation of the United States

National Committee for the Preservation of the Nubian Monuments. That was a formidable name, but it did state our purpose. I was already involved with another committee and knew that I would have to be out of the country frequently, to attend meetings in Egypt. So I spent the lunch hour campaigning for a slate of officers that did not carry my name. That was not very bright of me, because my efforts were rewarded by my election as executive secretary, the most time-consuming position. Brew was the obvious choice for chairman. William Stevenson Smith of the Boston Museum of Fine Arts and Froelich Rainey of the University Museum in Philadelphia were the first vice-chairmen. We were authorized to begin action.

One of the main tasks was publicity. The American people had to be informed that there was a clear and present danger in Nubia, but there was no justification for spending large sums of money on advertising. Fortunately newspapers and magazines saw it as a good story. *Reader's Digest* carried an excellent article early in the campaign, and other national magazines gave generous picture coverage. We scored one triumph. The able Minister of Culture of the U.A.R., Dr. Sarwat Okasha, came to this country with a portfolio of photographs showing antiquities that might come here as a traveling exhibit to publicize the Nubian emergency. We persuaded him that American museums already had objects fully as good as those offered, so that the exhibit would have no exceptional appeal. We asked for a selection of objects from the tomb of Tut-ankh-Amon, a name that would attract the public. Dr. Okasha was dubious because nothing from that famous tomb had ever left Egypt. He promised to present our appeal when he returned to Cairo, and he was successful. A modest but exciting group of Tut-ankh-Amon objects did tour the United States. It was the forerunner of those more sumptuous exhibits from the same tomb which later went to Tokyo, Paris, and elsewhere.

It seemed probable that the total Nubian campaign would cost at least $50,000,000. In my private mind I set the American goal at $20,000,000. That seemed outrageously high in contrast to archaeology's former appeals. Although I did not want to voice these ambitions unless we had some assurance of success, Senator Fulbright elicited the figure of $20,000,000 from me when I testified before the Senate Foreign Relations Committee. The figure was not impossible. Over the years the United States had sold to the United Arab Republic surplus grain amounting in purchase value to several hundred million of dollars. Under Public Law 480 this credit in purchase money remained in a debtor country, to be used for the mutual benefit of that country and of the United States. The huge sum in Egypt could easily stand the drain of $15,000,000 for the Nubian emergency.

Action to allocate American credits under Public Law 480 had to be taken in the House Appropriations Committee of our Congress, and on that committee were politicians who were implacably opposed to any official gesture for the benefit of an Arab government. However, the credit in Egypt had to be expended somehow. We hoped that these politicians would consider archaeology less offensive than military or economic assistance. The credit was in soft Egyptian pounds, which would apply to expenses inside Egypt. But the Nubian campaign would require hard American dollars also. We hoped to raise $5,000,000 here in hard money. My appeal to the big philanthropic foundations to start off such a drive was courteously shelved by them. It remained for a later and different committee, one specifically set up to aid in the rescue of Abu Simbel, to raise hard dollars up into seven figures.

The National Committee, operating without direct publicity or full-time staff, raised only many thousands of dollars. We had nearly a thousand responses to our soft approach, most of them for five or ten dollars, but accompanied by very cordial letters. There were heart-warming experiences, such as the letter from some grade-school children who had a hobby show and raised eighty-seven cents for Nubia. A schoolteacher sent in five dollars a month for nearly eight years. Hundreds wrote offering their services without pay. In the end I was the leading financial contributor. I took to the road in 1961–62 and gave eighty talks in fifteen months. Some of these were without fee, but I asked for an honorarium from any organization that seemed to be liquid, and any payments went into the Nubian account.

For large money the approach was to the Congress. Although I had testified before the Senate Foreign Relations Committee, our chief asset was Brew's experience in visiting senators and congressmen to urge the protection of American archaeological sites. In the spring of 1961, Brew, Edmundo Lassalle, a New York businessman, Prince Sadruddin Aga Khan of UNESCO, and I went to Washington. Sitting on a porch overlooking a pleasant park, we spent the morning writing proposals, criticizing them, and writing them over again until we had a workable document. In the afternoon we went to the White House and presented our appeal to President Kennedy's assistant, Richard Goodwin. He gave us a cordial reception and was sufficiently informed to question us closely. Our proposal was for $22,000,-000 out of the credits held in Egypt, of which $2,500,000 was to be applied to the removal of smaller temples in Egypt and the Sudan; $1,500,000 to aid American archaeological expeditions in the doomed country; $6,000,000 to save the temples of Philae; and we suggested a contribution of one-third rescuing the temples of Abu Simbel. That last portion appeared later to amount to $12,000,000. On April 6 President Kennedy sent a recommendation to the two Houses of Congress, with our carefully written proposals illuminated into eloquent appeal.

By 1971, $16,000,000 has been allocated as a result of President Kennedy's recommendation. How these allocations got through a busy and reluctant Congress is a story I know only by rumor and cannot detail here. Some congressmen have been willing to allow action if they did not have to go on record as supporting it. On two critical occasions the right formula was found. The $6,000,000 for Philae has not yet been brought again to the attention of Congress, because the plan to save Philae has not yet been clarified. The political climate is still unfavorable for effective action.

The United States National Committee for the Preservation of the Nubian Monuments is still in existence. South of the High Dam virtually all the excavations have long been completed. All the temples there that could be moved have been brought to safety. However, the Island of Philae lies north of the High Dam, and the actual rescue of the temples there is still in the future. The committee remains in existence in the hope that we may find some way of helping on that.

Early in 1960 I was invited to be a member of the Consultative Committee, set up under the auspices of UNESCO to advise the Egyptian Government about the archaeological work in Nubia and the rescue of the temples there. Bill Hayes had been the obvious American for that membership, but his health would not permit him to take on another obligation. Beginning in May of that year the committee met once or twice a year in Shepheard's Hotel in Cairo. A session would last from five to seven days.

I was still teaching in Chicago, and notice of a proposed meeting usually came only two or three weeks in advance. I had made rude remarks about other professors who went off on projects and left their students stranded. Now I was caught in my own criticism. I tried to make my absences as brief as possible, no more than ten days, with some lesson assignments for the students while I was away. This meant flying out to Egypt by jet plane—seventeen hours' travel time. The difference in time between Chicago and Cairo is eight hours. When the meetings began at 9:30 on the morning after my arrival, my biological-psychological system would protest that it was only 1:30 a.m. It usually took four days to adjust to the time differential.

When I returned to Chicago the reverse would be true. At a late morning class my system would demand that the working day end. The students had to be patient with a clod of a professor. On the evening after I had returned from one such trip I gave a public lecture. I warned the audience that it might be 8:30 in the evening for them, but that it was already 4:30 the next morning for me and this might be the first time that the lecturer fell asleep before his audience did. Although I did get through the lecture without flagging, the question period was a disaster. My befuddled mind refused to rise to the unforeseen demands made upon it.

It was difficult to think of the Cairo meetings as visits to Egypt. The sessions were held in a modern hotel, and we had little time to be out of doors. I was elected secretary for the committee, which meant that my spare time was spent in deciphering pencil notes taken on involved discussion and then setting them into parliamentary language for the minutes. If one is so imprisoned, it does not matter whether the meetings are in Cairo, Paris, or Chicago.

At the end of one meeting my thirty-year-old typewriter broke down finally and irreparably. Since I had registered its number for customs when I entered Egypt, I had to carry it to the airport for my departure. A new load of papers from the meetings now made my luggage overweight, and I asked for permission to abandon the typewriter at the exit customs. This was impossible. I had brought it in; I must take it out. I should not ask them to depart from established regulations. They finally did me the favor of not weighing it in with the rest of the luggage. I found that I should not be allowed to jettison it in flight or at any of the transit airports. I had to carry the corpse home with me before it could be consigned to its last resting place.

The Consultative Committee was carefully constructed in various ways. There were four Egyptians, one member from UNESCO, six from the West, and one from the Soviet Union. Counting them in a different way, there were five Egyptologists, two excavators of other cultures, one historian of art, one museum director, the Egyptian Minister for the High Dam, a representative of the Egyptian Ministry of Finance, and the deputy director-general of UNESCO. There were eleven men to one woman, but she was Mme. Noblecourt, who had been so influential in starting the whole Nubian campaign.

None of us knew in advance whether international politics would affect the discussions. Would there be an inflexible Egyptian or French or Russian or American attitude? But no one came charged by his government to defend national honor. Also, Fritz Gysin, the Swiss museum director, was elected chairman. He was an admirable presiding officer, understanding, patient, and firm. Almost all matters were argued and decided on their scientific merits. We agreed so well that a vote had to be counted on only one issue in all of the meetings.

Most members of the committee were, in some respect, official representatives of their home countries. But the Department of State had no formal interest in me as a member of this committee. I represented no academy or learned society. Nobody had briefed me on the proper American position about Nubian problems. The interplay of considerations had dictated that there should be an American on the committee, but officially I was *an* American, not *the* American. However, I could not convince some of my colleagues on the committee that my viewpoint was strictly my own. They would ask me what the American position on some question was. When I answered that I did not know, that I was serving the committee as an Egyptologist rather than as an American, some of them could not accept my statement because they came from so different a national setting.

At one time it seemed necessary to bring a technical expert from Rome to advise the committee on the chemical treatment of ancient materials. The representative from UNESCO said that there was no money for such a purpose. I burst into protest. If they would just let me take the round trip between Chicago and Cairo economy class instead of first class, they would save $500, which would be ample for the expenses of the man from Rome. Suddenly I was aware of a slight tension around the table. Some of my colleagues felt that they must do their countries justice by traveling in the dignity of first class. I hurriedly said that I was an exception, because my travel was more than twice as costly as that of any other member. It was agreed that less expensive arrangements should be made for me, and we did get the technical expert for the following meeting.

To be frank, airplane travel has become a bore. Without the constant attention from stewards and stewardesses that seems to be a feature of first class, I can read or sleep. Back in 1928, when I had my first bumpy flight in Germany, airplane travel was an exciting adventure. In the late 1930s, when one flew over lakes and mountains and farms or over those billowing clouds, flying offered beauty. Now it has simply become a means to go from one place to another without regard to pleasure or interest. When Mary and I flew from Thailand through Ceylon and India to Egypt, we spent half again as much time waiting in dreary airports for unaccountably delayed planes as we spent in actual flight. I have developed the same distaste for airports that my father had for railroad stations. But the alternatives of ocean liners or efficient railroad trains have nearly disappeared.

The twelve members of the Consultative Committee were assisted by Egyptian and UNESCO officials. The hotel room was crowded. At the first meeting the blast from the air-conditioner blew directly upon the interpreter, who could not change his seat. He developed a severe earache. From then on we did most of our own interpreting. The committee at first accepted French as the official international language, but much of the technical language was in English, and I found it difficult to render such terms as "riprap," "subsurface capillarity," and "grouting" into French. Five other members of the committee were more at home in English than in French. Only two lacked some English. We slowly forced the discussions into English, with translation into French or Russian when needed.

Professor Boris Piotrovski, the member from the Soviet Union, arrived for the first meeting with another Russian in attendance, introduced as his interpreter. This second man had only a little more English than his compatriot and almost no French. They always sat together and went together. It appeared that the interpreter had been sent along as a kind of consultant-governor for the member. Piotrovski had some command of German, and translation into that language satisfied him. He and I got along together in that medium. I had been studying Russian in preparation for the coming congress in Moscow in the summer of 1960. One morning the two Russians sat down beside me at the conference table. I greeted them with *zdravstvuite,* one of the few terms I had available. They responded to my "How do you do?" but looked startled and soon changed their seats. At the second meeting of the committee, Piotrovski was permitted to come alone. By the third and later meetings he was even allowed to join us in some of the evening social events. He was an able excavator and a friendly man.

A consultative committee can only advise. The Egyptian Government was under no obligation to accept our recommendations. They certainly wanted them and acted favorably on them as long as other conditions permitted, especially financial considerations. The committee inaugurated an archaeological survey of the two banks of the Nile in Egyptian Nubia, to establish priorities for excavation. The imminent deadlines made this a hasty operation. A team of young Egyptians and Englishmen made a heroic trek, foot-slogging 180 miles over rough terrain in search of important surface evidence. The committee set up standards of quality for excavation and epigraphy. It made recommendations on all applications for digging or copying in Nubia. There was only one case of two insistent bids for the same site. That was resolved on grounds of the competence of each party without vigorous protest from the losing group, which received another good location.

Most of us were experienced enough to handle the archaeological and epigraphic problems that faced the committee. However, the biggest question was one of engineering, the rescue of the two temples at Abu Simbel. About 175 miles south of Asswan a steep sandstone bluff faces the Nile. Shortly after 1300 B.C., Ramses II had two temples carved into this cliff. They were southern exponents for Egypt, majestically announcing to travelers north on the Nile that they were entering the domain of the great pharaoh. The temples are unique. Loss of them would be a confession of Egyptological indifference. But how do you preserve structures that belong to a single piece of hillside, with a façade nearly 100 feet high and with a penetration of 180 feet into the mountain? The four colossal figures of Ramses II that dominate the Great Temple are themselves 66 feet high. A Frenchman once said, "Imagine the Cathedral of Notre Dame carved out of a single block of stone!"

None of us would accept the argument that the engineering job was too difficult and too expensive, that the temples had been photographed, copied, and measured, so they could be allowed to sink under the waters of the new lake without loss to science. We felt that this would be an archaeological crime, like letting the stones of the Parthenon be burned for lime or using the Roman Forum as a quarry.

The obvious answer was to leave the temples in place and to protect them behind a coffer dam. That proposition was carefully studied by a French firm. We were at first disposed to accept their plan. But we were told that no dam is free from seepage and that the porous sandstone cliff drinks water thirstily. Pumps would have to work night and day to keep water out of the temples behind their lofty dam. If those pumps were to break down and repairs delayed for several days, the structures would be flooded. I entertained an aesthetic doubt also. The temples had been designed to be seen from the Nile, looming up in stately grandeur. If one had the first view of them from a boat moored above at a 160-foot dam, they would seem to shrink into insignificance inside a deep well. In the end the chief difficulty was that the estimated cost of the coffer dam started at $60,000,000 and went beyond $80,000,000 as revisions and higher costs appeared.

The alternative to a dam was a scheme so audacious that it inspired both ardent imagination and ardent fear. That plan was to cut each temple loose from the mountain in a single piece and to jack it 180 feet up in the air. After months of repeated tiny liftings, each structure would stand on steel and concrete pillars facing an artificial shore of the new lake. No engineer had ever lifted 250,000 tons before, and no one had ever attempted to raise a tremendous weight to such a height. Yet engineers were fascinated by the proposal and declared it entirely feasible. "It is simply a matter of extrapolation: if you need ten hydraulic jacks to lift 6000 tons, you use more than four hundred jacks to lift 250,000 tons." The Italian genius who devised this plan was gifted with daring and imagination. He was not equally gifted in making an estimate of costs. Here again the indicated amount was going above $80,000,000 when the proposal was dropped.

Debate over these two schemes came close to disturbing the harmony of the committee. Yet even though the proposal for a dam was called "the French plan" and that for elevation "the Italian plan," judgments were formed on professional grounds rather than along national lines. The archaeologists, except for myself, wanted to leave the temples in place behind a dam. The engineers and I wanted to lift them. This was the only time that we failed to reach a consensus by discussion, had to have a vote, and were obliged to report in our minutes that there was a difference of opinion. At other times we were united in what we called "the spirit of Nubia," a common eagerness to finish a stupendous job as quickly and as well as possible.

There may have been a little weariness when we finally accepted the so-called Swedish plan, which was to cut the temples into blocks, convey them to higher ground in trucks, and there reassemble them. We had given such intense concern to studying and supporting previous schemes that this slicing up of the structures seemed like an act of desperation. Despite assurances, we were not convinced that the friable sandstone would take kindly to sawing. Surely there would be considerable loss along the seams. With the wisdom of hindsight we can now see that this method has proved to be brilliantly successful.

The ultimate cost of the rescue of Abu Simbel was in the range of $40,000,000, of which the United Arab Republic paid more than half. I was sometimes confronted with aggressive questions: "Was it worth it?" or "Couldn't the money have been better spent on the needs of the modern world?" If the costs of the total Nubian campaign are measured against the costs of feeding hungry children on the one hand, or against the cost of a nuclear submarine on the other hand, the debate can be endless. Yet in defense one can say that for the things of the spirit—the great artistic achievements of man over the ages—there has never been so great and so successful a venture. At a time when the nations of the world were grimly competing with one another in military expenditures, they were able to agree on a cultural enterprise. This was a vigorous assertion that things of emotional and spiritual value go beyond mere price tags. Within the Nubian campaign Abu Simbel was the dramatic sign that men could still agree on cultural matters.

The Consultative Committee was not the only example of international cooperation. The archaeological expeditions in Nubia were also remarkably successful. A massive emergency welded the hastily constructed staffs into a harmonious unity. They had no tradition of the parochial jealousy that had characterized the 1920s. They visited one another and traded information about problems and techniques to achieve a common success. It was also a pleasure to see graduate students able to take the field. In the lean years between 1930 and 1960 few of them had had the opportunity to work in the area of their speciality. In archaeology, book learning is a poor substitute for the laboratory of unearthing new puzzles every day.

Although we should never have admitted it publicly, the full program of the Nubian campaign had seemed impossible at the start. That made the success all the more gratifying. Within a five-year limit not all of the temples could be saved, but eighteen of them, in whole or in part, were snatched to safety. That majestic monster, Abu Simbel, was reconstructed with skill. Not all of the excavation was carried out by experienced hands. Yet it was extraordinary that more than thirty expeditions from a score of different countries were able to take the field and to do a respectable job. Practically every one of the sites which that survey by young men had labeled as worth examining has been excavated. Not all of the rock inscriptions and drawings, a fascinating repertoire of graffiti, could be discovered and copied before the deadline. They often lay in out-of-the-way nooks. Yet hundreds of new ones were found and recorded. In all, there never before was so concerted and so comprehensive an archaeological activity.

By 1965 the task of the Consultative Committee had been completed. The remaining problems could be assigned to smaller teams. One team, composed of engineers, dealt with physical problems, the technical methods of cutting up the two Abu Simbel temples, transporting them, and rebuilding them in an artificial hill. I found myself a member of what was called the Landscaping Group. Although I might be able to distinguish between yew and rue or between sedge and hedge, my experience in landscaping was nil. The group was composed of three landscape architects and four Egyptologists.. Our responsibility was to make regular inspections of the work in the interests of historical accuracy and aesthetic setting. We were concerned with beauty and with truth, which should be the same thing in this reconstruction.

This assignment proved to be more interesting and more rigorous than the work on the Consultative Committee. Instead of being confined to a hotel room in Cairo, we held our meetings on trips to and from Abu Simbel. In congenial company that open-air excursion was a pleasure. Our government boat was no luxury liner, but it did get us from the High Dam to Abu Simbel and back, and we were too engrossed with our business to demand relaxed comfort. On the other hand, it was exhausting to scramble around a mountainside in summer temperatures. We were in session in the Abu Simbel rest house on one August afternoon when the temperature outside was 122 degrees Fahrenheit, and the air-conditioning apparatus was not working.

No reconstructed monument can ever look exactly like its original, but the façades and the interiors of the two temples are faithful to their former appearance. The visitor sees no marked sign of rebuilding. However, the cliff that enshrines the Great Temple is of necessity lower, because a monument built up out of cut blocks cannot carry the same weight as a solid hill. Therefore that façade does not seem to soar up as high as it used to. The cliff is also somewhat shorter in its southern extension. Some of the scenes and inscriptions carved into the rock surface have had to be put elsewhere or crowded together a little. That caused us much debate and regret that we could not present things just as they were three thousand years ago. The façades use the same stones in the same places as the original, and the seams between the blocks are very unobtrusive, so that the immediate framing of the two temples looks quite natural. The rest of the cliff is built up of random blocks of sandstone, graded away from the façades in quality of precision, so that there is some feeling of an artificial wall in the more distant setting of the façades. The consulting engineers who supervised the work tried various experiments to achieve a natural look. Try as they would, they never reached the ideal.

My Egyptian colleague from the Consultative Committee, Anwar Shoukry, was the Resident Archaeologist at Abu Simbel during the dismantling and reconstruction. His dogged insistence that carved surface be treated like delicate china and his determination to effect a true ensemble were blessings to the work. The Swedish consulting architects and the Italian quarrymen and masons were also the right men in the right places. The Italians treated stone with loving care. The success at Abu Simbel was made possible by those who worked there day by day, through heat and cold, through sandstorms and drought.

The Landscaping Group usually flew to Asswan and boarded the government steamer for the thirty-hour run to Abu Simbel. During meetings held in the cabin of the boat we agreed on the agenda, heard reports, and set up priorities of activity for our brief stop at the site. The actual stay at Abu Simbel might run between twelve and thirty hours, depending upon the demands of that particular inspection. As the boat returned to the High Dam we would thrash out our report.

We had some painful defeats. In the desire to achieve fidelity to the previous setting, it had been accepted that the floor of the small temple was to be exactly as much lower than the pavement of the great temple as it had been in antiquity. After the great temple was well along in its rebuilding, an administrative decision was made in Cairo to raise the height of the High Dam by a meter and a half. The small temple then had to be based at a slightly higher level. To be sure, no one will know this except ourselves. But when you are striving for exactness it is disturbing to have unexpected factors thwart your purposes. We wanted to have an ugly stone electric tower removed from the vicinity of the temples. We had to settle for a plantation of trees to mask its stark modernity.

Many tourists now visit Abu Simbel by the fast hydrofoil boats. The trip from the First Cataract takes five hours, they have about two hours to visit the temples, and then they have the five-hour return trip. The tourist boat is moored directly in front of the site, though we had recommended a harbor some distance away. The tourist would then have lost another half-hour of their visit in travel to and from the monuments. With grumbling, we had to accept this.

Abu Simbel deserves more than a two-hour visit. Since there is an adequate plane service to the site, a proper tourist schedule would be to fly from Asswan, spend twenty-four hours at Abu Simbel, and fly back the next day. Unfortunately a committee may propose, but a tourist agency will dispose.

Most of the group wanted to give the area that lonely, austere, and remote air that it once had as a distant holy place. However, it was soon made clear to us that the spectacle *Son et Lumière*, which presents a show of "Sound and Light" at night near the Sphinx (as well as at historic places in Europe and the United States), might be installed at Abu Simbel. Now it is all very well for tourists to make the evening journey from Cairo to Gizah to see a theatrical spectacle dramatizing the history of the Sphinx. They probably come to Gizah by day also, so that they may appreciate the ascetic sphinxlike character of the monument. But under present conditions most tourists come to Abu Simbel by hydrofoil and have about two hours there in the middle of the day. The *Son et Lumière* plan would make them a captive audience, behind closed doors, saluted by music, changing colors, and stentorian voices, moved from one room to another at command. The place would then be a noisy theater rather than a silent temple. Since it is assumed that tourists want a spectacle, the conflict between the asserted interests of archaeologists and the supposed interests of the general public will probably be resolved in favor of the entertainment extravaganza.

Son et Lumière insisted that wooden doors be installed at the entrance of each temple, so that the light inside could be controlled artificially. But one of the most exciting features of Abu Simbel was the penetration of the first rays of the sun, in spring and autumn, 180 feet into the Great Temple, to illuminate the sanctuary with the dawn light. At our 1971 meeting the group found that the wooden door interfered with this beautiful phenomenon and took away one of the functions of a temple that had been built to the sun god. We recommended that the upper part of the door be removed entirely. We preferred the showmanship of the ancient architects to modern theatrical variety.

The group has gone through some bitter debates on the best ways to reconstruct ancient monuments. But the leadership is good. The chairman is the Polish Egyptologist Professor Kazimierz Michalowski, and the secretary the Dutch Egyptologist Professor Adolf Klasens. They hold us together by infinite patience and firmness. Again, as in the case of the Consultative Committee, a common cause has cemented firm friendships. Again, English has been the common language, although the nationalities represented on the boat are Polish, Dutch, Egyptian, Italian, French, Danish, Swedish, and American. Before each evening meal some member usually produces a bottle of his national drink, and we toast all the heroes of that culture we can think of.

On the final evening before our return to the First Cataract the Secretary has to retire to the dining salon, where he and a typist hammer out the report for all to sign the next morning. The rest of us can relax. It has come to be a custom that I then recite some of the Arab folk tales that I have collected over the years—"The Three Blind Beggars," "The Cat Burglar," "Hajji Fatmeh and the Little Tailor," or tales about the Egyptian peasant Goha. When my English rendition of each story is finished, Louis Christophe, the representative from UNESCO, repeats it in French, with Gallic verve and gesture. It is such a good show that my colleagues do not tire of the same stories told twice a year. None of these tales appear in the formal record of the group, nor is there any account of our evening festivity.

Fifty years ago the life of an Egyptologist seemed to me a compound of copying texts, translating them, interpreting them in books, and teaching about them. Other calls and experiences have appeared, all of which have enriched my appreciation of the past and my feeling that the past and the present are both part of a single story.

FIFTEEN

TALES OUT OF SCHOOL

A PROFESSORSHIP in the Oriental Institute has continued to be a research position. The one obligation that the University of Chicago laid upon me was that I engage in "productive research," which was understood to be publication of books, articles, and reviews. I was like one of those tall fishermen on the Upper Nile, standing for hours in the water, perched upon one leg, with his spear poised to transfix a fish. However, the university knew that I had another leg, and there was a secondary obligation upon me to teach. If my performance on the two legs of research and teaching was satisfactory, the university was not concerned about the activities of my right hand inside the institution, in administration, student counseling, or committee memberships; or about the activities of my left hand outside the university in public lecturing, committeeships, or service jobs. These additional services should not interfere with the forward progress of research and teaching.

The requests from the public are many and varied. There are

letters from young people who believe that a good heart and a strong pair of shoulders are the only qualifications for field work and who offer themselves as unpaid volunteers for an excavation. It would cost more than $2000 to take them to and from the field and to maintain them there for six months. They would be of little use during the first season while they were being trained in methods and purposes. Such offers have to be declined. There are letters from schoolchildren who have to write a paper for class on the building of the pyramids and who ask that we send them "all information" on this subject. They are usually referred to an encyclopedia. There was a letter from a grade-school class who had taken the mummification of a guinea pig as their project and who wanted us to tell them the ancient Egypt method of embalming. The answer urged them to find other interests.

When the university switchboard receives telephone calls about Egyptological matters it will route them to one of us. Was Cleopatra very tall and fat with naturally red hair? No. Was the pharaoh Akh-en-Aton actually a woman masquerading as a man? No. Will "mummy wheat" germinate after thousands of years? Probably not. Are the Oriental rugs in a Midwestern museum from the tomb of Tut-ankh-Amon? No; that tomb had no such rugs, and the ancient Egyptians had no silk and would not use wool in their tombs. Did they have plywood in ancient Egypt? Yes. The volume of interest in that old culture remains high.

Visitors come to the university with antiquities they have purchased in Egypt or have found among the family possessions. For the most part these turn out to be of little value or are obvious forgeries. We deal sympathetically with these callers, because they often hope that their objects have a high commercial value, and there is always that outside chance that someone will bring in a unique treasure. We are more abrupt with those who bring in an "ancient Egyptian coin," with the picture of the sphinx and a pyramid on one side. That was made in 1893 as a souvenir of the "Streets of Cairo" at the Chicago World's Fair. Legally we are not appraisers for antiquities. We must decline to give an estimate of value, and our statements about the genuineness of an object are, for legal purposes, "informed opinions" rather than authentications.

In 1952–53, I had a research post in Egypt under the Fulbright program. The omens had not been favorable. "Black Saturday," when angry mobs took to the streets of Cairo and attacked Western installations, was only a few months past. King Faruq had been deposed in July 1952, and no one knew the attitude of the new military government. The year proved to be happily free and productive. I enjoyed cordial cooperation from all Egyptian officials. At the universities in Alexandria and Cairo I offered a brief series of lectures. Otherwise I was free to see those antiquities I had missed on previous visits. In particular I happily "went tombing," visiting at Gizah and Saqqarah the Old Kingdom mastabas, those oblong tombs with sloping sides beneath which lie the burial chambers.

In November, Mary and I had a ten days' stay in a house of the Antiquities Service in Saqqarah. In contrast to Chicago House at Luxor, the appointments were sparse—basic furniture, cutlery, and tableware. We rented linen and brought along a large assortment of food. The local market could supply only bread, eggs, milk, and some meat. Mary has always had an anthropological interest in the daily activities of people, and our house on the cliff overlooked a busy little village. We were so isolated that it was four days before we found out who had won the United States presidential election.

The local inspector gave me access to every monument I asked to see. I ultimately published "A Group of Sixth Dynasty Inscriptions" (*Journal of Near Eastern Studies,* 1954). J.-Ph. Lauer, the excavator and restorer of the complex around the Stepped Pyramid, took us down into its depths.

In December and January, together with Harold Nelson, we made an archaeological journey into the Sudan. Since we had specified goals in that country, the Sudan Government accepted us as a "scientific mission" and gave us special travel rates and residence in a government house at the Fourth Cataract. We were able to see nearly everything that we had planned for in our thirty days. We had to forego a visit to the pyramid area of old Meroë north of Khartum, because rains had made the roads very slick and our schedule allowed no leeway.

One special project was to copy certain texts housed in a little museum near the Fourth Cataract. This was in what was called "West Merowe" on the bank east of the Nile. In this region the river makes a long bend and flows toward the southeast instead of the north. Local custom insists that everything on the left bank is "west," even when it is east. More than thirty years earlier the Harvard–Boston Expedition under George Reisner had excavated here. Since the Boston Museum did not have complete copies of all the texts found, we had agreed to fill in the gap. We were the first residents in the Government Rest House there for more than a year. The accommodations were minimal but adequate, except that there was no refrigeration. The house man had to do each day's marketing in the early morning, when meat and fresh vegetables were brought in. After our early morning tea at six-thirty, he would go off to do his marketing, while we sat around until he returned. Breakfast might therefore be as late as nine o'clock. Since in January the midday Sudanese sun can blister the nose and crack the lips, we were anxious to start our work as early as possible, but we were caught by local custom.

After breakfast we would walk to the little museum. Our objectives were a huge granite sarcophagus of King Anlamani (about 600 B.C.) and some offering tables of King Si'aspiqa (about 475 B.C.). The offering tables could have been photographed and then treated in the Chicago House method of copying. The sarcophagus was another matter. It stood nearly 4 feet high and held about 330 square feet of tightly packed hieroglyphic inscription on a curved surface. Years earlier a British district commissioner had decided that these monuments should be made secure in so lonely a place. He had everything cemented firmly to the stone floor. Because the sarcophagus and its lid had inscriptions on their under surfaces, they were mounted on little stone pillars 13 inches high.

To do this huge copying job we fastened sheets of tough tissue paper to the stone surface with Scotch tape. Then we crumpled up carbon paper and massaged the tissue paper gently but firmly until the contours of the carved hieroglyphs sprang into sight. The sheets were then peeled off, numbered, and rolled up. We all started on the great outer surface, but after a time we left that area to Nelson. Mary got a chair and climbed inside the huge vessel to rub the texts there. My stint was the underside, that surface fixed just 13 inches above a cold stone floor. I would worm my way in, fasten the tissue paper with Scotch tape and curses, and then try to rub with the crumpled carbon paper, all this about 3 inches away from my nose. We all had blue fingers for days afterward. I had also a clown's appearance, with a blue nose and streaks across my face. When we returned to Khartum, Nelson mailed 125 sheets of rubbings to Boston. The inscriptions were of some importance. They were versions of the Pyramid Texts, which had assumed form in Egypt more than a thousand miles to the north and nearly two thousand years earlier. These old Ethiopian kings clung fiercely to tradition.

Near the Fourth Cataract there are several temples and many pyramids. We tried to see all of them. We planned to spend a full day on the "east side," to see the pyramid fields of Gebel Barkal and Kurru, and the assistant district commissioner ordered the ferryman to take us over at eight or eight-thirty. But that morning our breakfast was unusually late, and when we reached the riverbank the ferry had already crossed to the opposite shore. It returned and fetched us, but by now the sun was high. We hurried to our sightseeing.

While our party was at Gebel Barkal we were summoned back to the riverbank. There we witnessed that extraordinary phenomenon of river-talking. On each bank a man stood beside the water, facing down toward the water, and shouted in long-drawn-out tones. This carried remarkably well over long distances. The message was that the assistant district commissioner had learned that the ferryman had disobeyed orders by not waiting for us. The miserable fellow had been placed in chains and was under arrest awaiting our reaction as to his punishment. We begged for his release. Not only were we the ones who had been late, but he was the only ferryman and we wanted to be sure that we could get back at the end of the day. When we were ready to go back, he was there waiting for us. He even refused to let a farmer take across a cow and a donkey, so that the distinguished visitors might have the old boat all to themselves.

We were in Khartum over Christmas and attended the last British holiday in the Sudan before the country became a republic. The Grand Hotel laid on a magnificent Christmas Eve dinner. Officials came in from all over the country, bringing their families or meeting children who came out from England for the holiday. Some appeared in formal evening dress, and some were just able to make it, still dressed in singlets and khaki shorts. There was a shade of cloud over the festivities. After half a century the British were leaving the Sudan. The Empire was shrinking.

Later, when we were in the Wadi Halfa Hotel on our return trip, we had a visit from the British district commissioner. This might have seemed an unusual honor, but we found that he wanted to ask a favor of us. They could have an Anglican church service on Sunday only if the congregation came to more than ten. The resident British numbered about right, but occasionally some of them were absent or were detained on business. If Harold Nelson, Mary, and I would be kind enough to come, they would be sure of the required number. Of course we were glad to do so. It was a melancholy occasion. There was no clergyman. The district commissioner himself conducted the service, and a man from the airport read the lesson. We sang

lugubriously without benefit of an organ. But we were happy
that we had helped to maintain a tradition that was important to
our hosts. They were clinging to the past with some of the same
intensity as the old Ethiopian pharaohs did.

A very different adventure was the case of the Joseph Smith
papyri. When the Latter-day Saints were in Ohio in 1835 an
Englishman visited them and exhibited four Egyptian mummies,
together with at least four rolls of papyrus and hypocephalus. (A
hypocephalus is a circular sheet of papyrus stiffened with plastered linen, on which is inscribed excerpts from The Book of the
Dead; it was laid under the head of a mummy of late times in
Egypt). The Mormons purchased this collection. Joseph Smith
set himself to studying the hieratic texts on the papyri and the
cursive hieroglyphic on the hypocephalus, with a view to translating them.

Nobody in the United States could read Egyptian in 1835.
Jean-François Champollion's decipherment of Egyptian based on
the Rosetta stone had been announced only a few years earlier
and was still not finally accepted in Europe. The Englishman had
been told that the only man in America who might read those
texts was in Ohio: Joseph Smith had achieved his prophetic fame
by his translation of the golden tablets of Mormon, published in
1830. He worked patiently on the new material now. He came
to the conclusion that one of the rolls was the writing of Abraham and another the writing of Joseph while the Israelites so-
journed in Egypt.

If I understand the Mormon account of Joseph Smith's different translations, the rendering of the golden tablets flowed easily,
whereas that of the papyri was laborious. In the former case inspiration came automatically, and he sat behind a curtain dictat-
ing a translation directly to his scribes. But he toiled for months
over the Egyptian documents, slowly working out a "Grammar
& Alphabet of the Egyptian Language" (reproduced in 1966 by
the Modern Microfilm Co., Salt Lake City). In 1842 he issued a

little book, *The Pearl of Great Price*, containing his interpretation of some of the material. There is some contrast between the two translations. A Gentile might believe that the force of inspiration was more labored in the case of the Egyptian documents. But the definition of inspiration is a subject that belongs to the field of theology.

Now, well over a century later, we can check the story of the two renderings. According to his account, Joseph Smith was empowered by the use of supernatural eyeglasses to make his direct dictation to his assistants for the golden tablets. He labored on the Egyptian material out in the open, without the benefit of unusual spectacles. When he decided that he had the Book of Abraham, the little pictures in the papyri conformed to his understanding. What Egyptologists take to be a scene in which a dead Egyptian stands before Osiris, the god of the dead, was for Joseph Smith a picture of Abraham in the presence of Pharaoh. What Egyptologists see as the god Anubis embalming a corpse, he declared to be "the idolatrous priest of Elkenah attempting to offer up Abraham as a sacrifice." What Egyptologists accept as individual hieratic groups or words became for him full paragraphs as written by the Biblical patriarch; thus the word "great" was developed by Joseph Smith into a paragraph in which Abraham told how he was rescued from sacrifice: "And as they lifted up their hands, upon me, that they might offer me up, and take away my life, behold I lifted up my voice, unto the Lord my God, and the Lord hearkened and heard, and he filled me with a vision of the Almighty and the angel of his presence stood by my feet and immediately loosed my bands." This was derived from the text that we shall refer to below as "the Breathing Permit." When Joseph Smith called the text the writings of Abraham about his sojourn in Egypt, it acquired a prophetic quality that ranked it just below the Book of Mormon in divine inspiration for the Latter-day Saints.

The Mormons moved from Ohio to Illinois. There the Gentiles attacked the community, killed Joseph Smith, and, according to an accepted account, appropriated the Egyptian material. This report went on to claim that the mummies were exhibited in St. Louis, then moved to a museum in Chicago, where they perished in the 1871 fire. Presumably the papyri and the hypocephalus were burned up with them.

That was what I understood in 1964 when I was working on the manuscript of *Signs and Wonders upon Pharaoh*. However, a friend told me that he had learned that some of the documents were still in existence, although he was not permitted to tell me where they were. So I altered the text, which later appeared on p. 38, to insert the words that are here given in italics: "the Egyptian pieces were carried off to a museum in Chicago, *according to the story*. When the great fire swept that city in 1871, these texts with their curious history were *allegedly* destroyed." That was the best that I could do under the confidential terms of the information given me.

In May 1966 Professor Aziz Atiya of the University of Utah, looking over Coptic manuscripts in the Metropolitan Museum of Art in New York, discovered some of the Joseph Smith papyri. They were not all present. The mummies and the hypocephalus were still missing. In November 1966 the museum turned the pieces over to the Church of the Latter-day Saints. From an old bill of sale that went along with the papyri it appeared that certain Egyptian pieces had been in Mormon possession until 1856, when they were sold privately. By inheritance they ended up as the property of a lady in Brooklyn, and then they were purchased by the Metropolitan Museum in 1947. When they went to Utah the most important pieces had come home again after obscure wanderings.

The transcriptions of the stained papyri which Joseph Smith had published in different places were not always legible. Scholars in the past had been unable to get any running translation from these copies. Now it would be possible to examine the texts more closely. However, the matter might be delicate. Back in 1912 an Episcopal bishop had mounted an attack on Joseph

Smith as a translator. He had solicited and published several off-hand and hostile opinions from Egyptologists. The resulting controversy had left a lot of bitterness. Scholarship required a more responsible analysis than a lot of indignant snorts.

The opportunity came in 1967. The editors of *Dialogue: a Journal of Mormon Thought* invited several American Egyptologists to accept photographs of the documents and to comment on them from their professional standpoint. They wanted to know what Gentile scholars thought about these treasures of the church. Although I expressed the gruff opinion that photographs were a poor substitute when the originals were available and that proper method would require handling the actual papyri, detaching them from their cloth backing, and then sorting the separate pieces into their proper place, I did accept the invitation. I presented a summary report on the longest papyrus in the Summer 1968 issue of *Dialogue*. The document was identified as a standard Book of the Dead of late times (well after 300 B.C.), executed for a lady Ta-shere-Min, whose mother was Nes-Khonsu. Although now cut up into ten pieces, it had once been a scroll of noble length, perhaps 10 feet or more. The little illustrations for each chapter of the Book of the Dead were abstractions, in which the lady's face was a blob and her arms were matchsticks. Yet they had a certain elegance. Ta-shere-Min sowed grain or paddled her little skiff in the next world with compact neatness.

In the following issue of *Dialogue* (autumn 1968), my colleague Klaus Baer did a more incisive job. His article was entitled "The Breathing Permit of Hor. A Translation of the Apparent Source of the Book of Abraham." This was another late papyrus. Its magical force was to allow the deceased person to breathe the breath of life in the next world. This text was not as common as the Book of the Dead, but several other papyri of "the Breathing Permit" are known, all of Roman times. Baer translated what was extant of this document. As a matter of course, he pointed out that three pieces Joseph Smith had translated as having unusual significance were, from the standpoint of the Egyptologist, incorrectly mounted in their present position and thus meaningless in their assumed context. In the Book of Abraham these three fragments were translated to state that the descendants of Ham were under a curse and could not ascend to the priesthood. On this basis blacks could be accepted into the Church of the Latter-day Saints, but they could not have that full role expressed by the priesthood. Not only did Egyptological study disagree with Joseph Smith's translation, but it even was pointed out that the pertinent fragments were out of place in the remainder of the so-called Book of Abraham.

In agreeing to study the papyri we had no interest in controversy. We simply were eager to try out our skills on new manuscripts. I should not have agreed to translate if the invitation had not come from the Mormons.

Mormon theologians have mounted a counterattack against our translations. In a series of articles published in 1968–69 in the magazine *Improvement Era,* Dr. Hugh Nibley pointed out at some length that Egyptologists differed in their interpretations of the material upon which they worked. He therefore suggested that we were unreliable. In every field, be it physics or medicine or economics, scholars emphasize their disagreements and take their agreements for granted. A slight discordance is exaggerated whereas the general concordance is ignored. In this case Egyptologists may disagree as to whether the trace left at the edge of a break shows fingers of a man's hand or feathers of a flying bird's wing, but they will all agree that we have here normal ancient Egyptian Books of the Dead and a normal "Breathing Permit."

A valid counterargument for the faithful would be that we Egyptologists can claim no inspiration. We can only scrape the surface meaning. If Joseph Smith was a prophet, he was an instrument of divine authority, so that he might find the deepest meaning. Although our work deals with fact, we must respect faith. As the Protestant world survived the Higher Criticism of the Bible three generations ago, the Mormons will survive this criticism.

SIXTEEN

THE YEARS OF JUBILEE

More than four thousand years ago an Egyptian prime minister said to his king: "O sovereign, my lord! Oldness has come; old age has descended. Feebleness has arrived; dotage is coming anew. The heart sleeps wearily every day. The eyes are weak, the ears are deaf, the strength is disappearing because of weariness of heart, and the mouth is silent and cannot speak. The heart is forgetful and cannot recall yesterday. The bone suffers old age. Good is become evil. All taste is gone. What old age does to men is evil in every respect. The nose is stopped up and cannot breathe. Simply to stand up or to sit down is difficult" (*Ancient Near Eastern Texts*, edited by James B. Pritchard, 1969).

This official was asking that his son be promoted to serve as his successor. He may have exaggerated his senility. Perhaps he was no more than fifty years old. From the standpoint of three score years and ten he might appear to be a man in the prime of life. Yet there is still a lot of truth in his complaint. Universities make a professor an emeritus at sixty-five or, more rarely, at seventy. Quite properly he should give way to younger men. Yet there may still be a little resentment at being put on the shelf. I prefer the Spanish term for retirement, *jubilación*, with the professor turned out to pasture called a *jubilato*. That means that the man has reached the Biblical age of jubilee, the release of the servant. It implies a happier future than our terms.

It is hard to stop a career at midnight on some designated day, and the University of Chicago has been very generous to me. At the statutory age of sixty-five I was put on "deferred retirement," which meant that I might have three more years as a kind of decompression chamber, slacking off on the work load. Teaching was to be at my own volition, and there was no obligation to serve on committees. A crisis in the department summoned me to teach the late period of Egyptian history, a subject I had neglected for many years, and this was a refreshing challenge. Meanwhile I chose to teach language courses in the autumn and spring quarters and to spend the winters in Egypt. What could have been greater cause for jubilation?

Best of all, I was now available for field work. In 1966 Professor Walter Fairservis, then of the University of Washington, proposed to start an excavation at Hierakonpolis, about fifty miles south of Luxor. This famous place offered material from the end of prehistory and the beginning of history. The Antiquities Service in Egypt did not know Fairservis personally or the members of his proposed staff. They asked that the expedition include someone with a name they could recognize. Unhappy experience with some fly-by-night excavators had made them want to focus responsibility for any expedition. Fairservis invited me to join the team. I protested that I had never been a dirt archaeologist, that I could offer no expertise to an expedition that might find few hieroglyphic inscriptions, and that I had already committed myself to a program of study in the library of Chicago House at Luxor. These reservations were swept aside. What he wanted was a consultant who could make occasional visits to Hierakonpolis and serve as a sounding board for problems and ideas. If I were based at Chicago House I could come on short notice. That sounded like a privilege. To be sure, the Antiquities Service might look upon me as the responsible person if anything went wrong. However, I knew the members of the expedition well enough so that I anticipated no trouble. I accepted, happy that I was so easily available.

At Hierakonpolis the point of interest was a low mound lying in the cultivated fields, known to be of earliest dynastic times, and there was also a great churned mass of predynastic and early dynastic pottery on the desert margin. The ancient Egyptians had treated the place as a holy area from their oldest times. The expedition had the two seasons of 1966–67 and 1968–69 in the field. In each year I made two visits of a few days each.

Hierakonpolis was sampled at the end of the nineteenth century and yielded unique material—the slate palette of King Nar-mer and the copper statue of King Pepi I, now in the Cairo Museum. For the next three generations archaeologists cast covetous eyes on the site, but the sprawling place was too large and too complex to undertake in a season or two.

On my first trip Walter Fairservis telephoned me at Chicago House and said he thought I should come and see what they had. I asked what did they have. He answered, "We've found a wall." I burst into laughter: walls are the skeleton of archaeology and are found everywhere. It turned out that their wall was exceptional. The full extent of this massive structure of mud brick has still not been traced.

Going to Hierakonpolis was always an adventure. I took the train from Luxor to the Edfu station. Then there was a slow crossing of the river by the smoky, crowded little ferry. At the other side I had to fend off the guides who wanted to show me the Edfu temple, and then I had to bargain for a horse carriage to take me to the taxi stand. At the taxi stand I had to bargain again, for the trip to Kom el-Ahmar, the modern name for the mound at Hierakonpolis. No drivers ever seemed to know this place, so they set a correspondingly high price to compensate for their ignorance. Not until my fourth trip did I learn to specify the village of Muissat, about three miles away from Kom el-Ahmar. It was a twelve-mile drive along a tree-shrouded embankment, and we invariably shot past the narrow little dike that led to the mound and had to turn around and come back. These contingencies were so common that the Hierakonpolis staff had learned never to look for a visitor until he actually arrived.

What I have learned is that archaeology is a more responsible profession than it was forty years ago. Certainly the earlier diggers were serious enough about their work, but to a large extent they played it by shrewd hunches. It is remarkable that their hit-or-miss tactics hit more often than they missed.

Attitudes and techniques follow rules more rigidly. Seventy years ago Flinders Petrie laid down the dictum that everything found in excavation is evidence and must be given careful consideration. This has advanced to the point where any eccentric find that defies a reasonable explanation is a focus of attention, no matter how insignificant it is materially. What would you make of a clutch of eleven stones carefully laid together on a ledge, each one about the size and shape of an ostrich egg? It should have meaning since they were deliberately gathered together in one spot. Much puzzling has been devoted to them, even though a solution will probably not change history. So far there has been no answer to the problem of such stones in their setting. If they were weights of some kind, why should they be given such careful treatment?

One day in 1967 I was sitting watching the others pursue the intricate problems of their plots of earth. To make myself useful, I climbed the western cliffs to scout for indications of ancient tombs. I was so happy to be busy in the field again that I gamboled from one rocky outcrop to another like a young goat. The result was a muscle sprain in my back. Later that spring Mary and I had to forego a proposed visit to Iran while I had heat therapy in a hospital. The lesson in this is that archaeology is a young man's game. Scrambling in and out of pits, crouching over some new find, or bracing oneself against a driving sandstorm are all part of the job for the young and vigorous. I should have played the role of a village elder, sitting solemnly in the market place where the populace could come to him for counsel. That seemed too presumptuous, but I paid for the other presumption of thinking that I was still young.

Egyptologists can go on digging the sites of historical times and thus add to the evidence for the better-known periods. However, the better goal may be the lesser-known times, particularly that important transition from prehistory into history, the period of the late predynastic and the beginnings of the dynasties. One mound at Hierakonpolis contains a sacred enclosure of the Old Kingdom; in another huge mound the potsherds indicate that there were burials from predynastic into dynastic. On the cliffs up a western *wadi* there are Middle and New Kingdom tombs of the local nobles. Ancient Egyptian tradition cherished Hierakonpolis at the south and Buto at the north as the two sacred places of its own antiquity, which goes back into important primitive times. Buto in the Delta is waterlogged in its early levels. Hierakonpolis promises the excavator critical material for the understanding of the transition into civilized life.

Although I had read about some of the new techniques, it was impressive to see them in practice. There was a new expert, a geomorphologist, from Austria. He was trained to recognize the contour and texture of soils and gravels, thus establishing where ancient man had lived or had grown crops. What the ordinary observer might pass over as gravel of a slightly different color or composition appears to him as the decomposition of agricultural fields or of a village street that existed five thousand years ago. The geomorphologist found a settlement up what is now a dry *wadi*, far away from any current sources of irrigation. The pottery specialists then moved in and picked up sherds that could be dated as predynastic of a respectable antiquity. An excavator would probably have found the site only by accident, for he would not consider it possible for a farming settlement to be so far out in the desert.

The presence of an agricultural settlement, no matter how small, so far away from water is a puzzle. We make categorical statements about the Egyptians being entirely dependent upon the Nile inundation and what water they might retain from it. The geomorphologists, climatologists, and geologists may revise our thinking. Was ancient man much more skillful in trapping what water there might be from rains, which were a little more regular than at the present day? I once wrote an article (*Journal of Near Eastern Studies* 1955) claiming that Hierakonpolis must have been small and economically insignificant because it lay in an area that is poor in its modern agricultural production. That may have been reasonable as a theory, but actual observation has shown that I was wrong.

Any ancient mound is first surveyed and then sectioned into squares, perhaps ten meters on a side. For example, Square H-7 would be located by pegs at each corner, lettering from A onward from the west and from 1 onward from the north. If there is adequate surface evidence, excavation may begin with those squares that look the most promising. One digs slowly down, recognizing by hard-packed or burned floors the successive levels. If the surface evidence does not point clearly to the best sections, a trial trench may be run right through the mound until it meets the best-looking pay dirt. At Hierakonpolis the director assigned squares to himself and to four of his staff. Each was responsible for careful supervision of his sector and for pushing or slowing up the work as the finds might indicate.

In every dig in the Near East pottery has been the key material. Jewelry or valuables were probably picked up in antiquity. Wood was too valuable to leave. Stone was picked out for reuse. But kitchen utensils or tableware of pottery could not be reused, was universally common, and often was left where it stood or was broken. Pottery changed recognizably from century to century. As the most common material that may be typed, it has therefore become the means of dating in rough terms. What we call Amratian pottery is known to be older than Gerzean, which is older than dynastic. One does not need a whole pot, however much one would like that. Broken sherds are far more common and work nearly as well for dating purposes.

One simple technique in excavation is what the jargon of the trade calls a "statistical profile." Let us say that we are finding Ware A, a rather soft, brown ware, Ware B, a coarse buff ware, often with a wavy ledge on the shoulder, and Ware C, a firm pottery with a polished red surface. We might then pick one section of the mound where no important buildings are visible and dig a square in arbitrarily fixed levels of uniform depth. Let us say that the result is:

	Number of Sherds		
Depth	*Ware A*	*Ware B*	*Ware C*
0–20 cm.	75	30	5
20–40 cm.	30	50	35
40–60 cm.	5	40	70

As a mound builds up, the top level is the most recent and the lower levels are progressively older. The sampling above shows that Ware A is the most recent and that Ware C is the oldest, with B overlapping both. The statistical profile may be reversed, because we know from the digging of others that the time sequence runs C, B, and finally A. Since the mound at Hierakonpolis was a sacred area for many centuries, there might have been some rebuilding, which would have churned up the soil and provided reversals of the normal order. This profile therefore shows that there has been no abnormal upsetting of the levels in the process of rebuilding.

One particular square was rich in broken pottery. It may have been part of the village dump. An ingenious young member of the expedition was interested in how garbage and trash were disposed of five thousand years ago. He came to the conclusion that soft garbage was simply dropped almost anywhere—on the village street or the floor of a house. However, hard debris would have been uncomfortable to walk on, and apparently was carried away from the house to the village midden and thrown upon the pile accumulating there. The dump contained potsherds, broken stone vessels and grindstones, and other hard trash. As far as I know, nobody before had asked this question about disposal. It can hardly be glorified as municipal sanitation, but it does illustrate an ancient response to a problem underfoot.

Organic material that was turned up was saved for analysis of its radioactive carbon content, an accepted means of rough dating. For material from the beginning of the dynasties, about 3000 B.C., the carbon-14 dating is a useful check, but it does not provide the precision of a single century. Pottery still remains the essential sequence control running from one period to another, as it did seventy years ago.

Human and animal bones were saved for later laboratory identification. Samples of earth at different levels were taken, to be analyzed for a count of the pollen imbedded in the soil, which gives an index of the quantity and nature of the floral life of the periods.

The Hierakonpolis expedition had planned to have a botanist, but none was available with the interest and expertness in ancient plants. There were other new tricks, publicized for their success elsewhere, that could not be applied at Hierakonpolis. Dendrochronology, the charting of the growth of tree rings year by year and the resultant ability to date a timber with precision, has not yet been brought to the Near East. In Italy and Greece archaeologists have adapted a device already used for the discovery of deposits of petroleum: an electrical impulse is sent down and the echo from stone structures underground is recorded. The mud-brick buildings on the mound at Hierakonpolis would not respond to this technique. Over the past fifty years the staffing of an excavation has changed as the methodology has changed. Pottery remains centrally important, as does architecture, but the historian-philologist has given way to the expert in organic and inorganic materials.

To my inexperienced eye the detection of a mud-brick wall lying in the context of a mound of accumulated mud is still something of a miracle. On one of my visits I found Fairservis and the head foreman crouched down on their haunches, debating whether a wall of mud bricks was actually making a curve or not. Were the workmen following an ancient circular surface, or were they now imaginatively carving bricks into a wall that had never existed? It was decided to follow the apparent curve. This decision was correct. Just a little way around the bend there appeared a bed of ashes. This had accommodated itself to the rounded surface of ancient times, proving that the workmen had been right. What they were excavating was a round kiln or storage pit.

The daily process of digging is pretty much what it was fifty years ago. Local villagers move the earth under the immediate supervision of Guftis, those workmen from the Upper Egyptian town of Guft, who are now in their fourth or fifth generation as trained diggers. The Westerner, with his notebook and camera, watches at the top of the pit or scrambles down to check some new appearance. On a hot day the work moves by fits and starts. Sometimes a song leader starts an antiphonal chant, and the laborers respond to his theme. Then they bestir themselves actively to the beat of the song. After it is over they return to slow motion.

There was one new factor at Hierakonpolis. It used to be that practically all workers were illiterate, and they would sign the payroll with a thumb print or a brass signet. The 1968–69 season started out with a majority of illiterates. Their more learned companions jeered at them, until within a few weeks most of them had learned to sign their names. This ambition and this personal pride are factors of modern Egypt, giving a promise for the future of the land.

The Western staff member watches the moving of earth carefully. When a complete pot or a skull appears, he goes down into the pit with a knife and a brush to assist a Gufti foreman in the delicate removal. The supervision is more constant than in the past. An excavator no longer retreats to his tent for an hour to work at his notes. Notes are for the evening. As long as earth is being moved, he is in close attendance. In the past photography might be invoked only for the exceptional discovery. Now it is constant, and the twelve-foot wooden tripod for a vertical view is standard equipment. Archaeology destroys, in the sense that it removes objects from their context. The recording of every location and every association is important for the record. Anyone who has tried to make sense out of field notes made fifty years ago knows how vital these details are. It is better to have too much record than too little, as the future may ask questions not considered at the time of discovery.

At Hierakonpolis a large pot was found, mouth down into an ancient floor. Two staff members dug out the earth around this, strengthened the surface with strips of adhesive tape, and carefully lifted it out. It contained the remains of an infant. Later a similar pot was found, and the field director jokingly said that this would be called "the Wilson pot." It was removed with the same care. The most minute sifting of the contents showed nothing in it but earth. The staff was somewhat embarrassed for me. I took it as a useful lesson about overexpectation.

Forty years ago the Egyptian Government gave a foreigner a concession to dig a specified area and then left him alone until the division of the finds at the end of his season. That expressed the more patrician opportunities of the Westerners at that time. It also expressed the looser controls of the past. Now an Egyptian inspector is assigned to each expedition, and he is in daily attendance. The guest excavator and the Antiquities Service have a mutual responsibility. To be sure, the character of the inspector is an unforeseeable problem. A city boy who is homesick and bored out in the provinces or a boy who is defensive against foreigners may present difficulties. Westerners who express a feeling of superiority to "these natives" do not help relations. But a young Egyptian who wants to make archaeology his career may enter into the spirit of the work with enthusiasm. The inspector at Hierakonpolis had his own square to dig and was a part of the staff socially.

For the first season the expedition was quartered in the Edfu Hotel and had to make the twelve-mile trip, with all their equipment crowded into a taxi, each day. The second season they had a comfortable houseboat moored at the riverbank three miles from the mound. The group was young and blessed with a combination of enthusiasm and businesslike methodology. They were much better trained than we had been at their age. Five nationalities were represented, but there was little of that polite wariness common on mixed digs of the past. The running series of little personal jokes was most intense at the expense of the youngest American man, but democratically included everybody and was enjoyed by everybody.

The women were partners rather than handmaidens. Earlier digs had included an occasional woman archaeologist of exceptional ability, but the men had looked upon her with a mixture of awe and derision. Now it was taken as a matter of course that a girl should have a square to excavate under her supervisory control. In the tight little community of a staff out in the lonely provinces, men might still prefer to be associated with men, rough and tough, as the work is rough and tough. But women have proved themselves so good that the staffing of an expedition now seeks them out. That weariness of spirit and that testiness of disposition which descend upon all expeditions at the end of a season affect women too, but everybody is aware of the situation and stands up under it.

Field expeditions in the Near East show another change over

the past two generations. The field director used to be the absolute authority. Often he was the only experienced person on the expedition. His assistants were students or volunteers. In any case, they became his disciples. The pattern was set by Flinders Petrie, the father of controlled archaeology. He directed all available funds to digging rather than to living conditions, and his staff would endure the most burdensome austerity without rebellion. If the master made an apparent mistake, they did not question it because he must have had his reasons. Later his assistants might ruefully exchange reminiscences about their harsh experiences, but they would not admit to the outside world that there was a flaw in this master of masters. In general, that pattern of absolute authority descended to field directors after Petrie, such as Reisner and Borchardt and Winlock. In these days of professional specialization it is no longer possible to treat the field director as omniscient and infallible. He has to rely upon experienced technicians rather than upon unskilled amateurs. No field dig could run without a court of last appeal, and the field director must still have that final word. But since he has become the leader of independent-minded craftsmen, he can succeed only if he respects the opinions of his staff members.

The transition to a limited monarchy has not been easy. Independence of mind within a unit that needs some daily discipline can be dangerous. During the Nubian campaign there were expeditions, hastily constructed in staff, where the authority of the field director was challenged by some ambitious specialist. Intensity of work within a limited time may produce an intensity of personal feeling. The field director will find that his speech from the throne must be written in part by members of his cabinet. He has to live with his people twenty-four hours a day.

Political crises have hampered the progress of the Hierakonpolis work. The expedition did not take the field in the season after the 1967 war between Israel and the United Arab Republic. Then after the 1968–69 season the Egyptian security forces declared such rural areas as Hierakonpolis out of bounds to foreigners. The site is so important that one hopes for an early peace in which archaeology may again have that undivided attention which the field worker offers.

In 1969–70 I joined a very different project. To explain its purpose I must set the ancient background. About 1370 B.C. the fourth of the pharaohs carrying the name Amen-hotep became king of Egypt. His wife was Nefert-iti. Modern commentators have heatedly called him the world's first monotheist, first individual, first doctrinaire, and first prig. He began his reign honoring the imperial god Amon and ruling from Memphis and Thebes, as his predecessors had done. By his time Egypt had enjoyed a century of wide imperial rule, wealth, and prestige. The traditional bases of the culture were being affected by alien influences. The king began to focus his worship upon the sun god, under the name of Re-Harakhte. In his sixth year he broke sharply with the religious politics of the past, changed his name from Amen-hotep to Akh-en-Aton, began the worship of the sun disk, called the Aton, and moved his capital to a place in Middle Egypt that we call Tell el-Amarna. This sharp change is known as the Amarna Revolution.

While the king was still at Thebes he started one temple in the traditional art, dedicated to the sun god Re-Harakhte. This he seems to have abandoned abruptly. In a very short time he initiated a new art and architecture at Thebes, and at Karnak he erected a huge temple for the jubilee of himself and his new god. Its scenes were executed in the feverish new art, which permitted an exaggeration of the human form approaching caricature. Work on the decoration of this temple continued even after Akh-en-Aton had abandoned Thebes and moved to Amarna. The building stones were relatively small in size, only one cubit—that is, about twenty and a half inches—in length. For some reason that eludes us, modern Egyptian workmen call them *talatat*, "threes." They are much smaller than the usual temple blocks. Just as Akh-en-Aton's art concentrated upon his own day, instead of upon eternity, so his architecture was not solid and lasting.

Shortly after the death of Akh-en-Aton, his son-in-law Tut-ankh-Amon was forced to return to Thebes and to the older religion and politics. The worship of the Aton became a heresy. After Tut-ankh-Amon had died men began to pull down the Karnak temple of Akh-en-Aton. The *talatat* were carried off and piled inside the Second and Ninth Pylons of the temple of Amon at Karnak, as the inner stuffing. To a lesser degree they were so employed elsewhere, hidden for centuries inside massive structures. Akh-en-Aton's temple was thus lost to sight until modern times.

Just before the twentieth century parts of the temple of Amon at Karnak began to collapse because of inadequate foundations, which were affected by a higher water table. Repair and recon-solidation became annual obligations. In the late 1920s and in the 1930s hundreds of *talatat* were discovered under the floor of the Hypostyle Hall and inside the Second Pylon. They were stacked up in the Karnak temple enclosure until someone could sort them out and put them together again.

By the 1960s it was clear that the known *talatat* would number more than thirty thousand. That estimate applied only to those carved with scenes and inscriptions. They were so numerous, had been so dispersed in their architectural location, and had so many recurrent elements that it proved to be impossible to re-construct them by eye alone. While they were standing stacked out in the open, the blocks lost some of their surface paint and a number of them disappeared, apparently into the European antiquity markets.

These blocks constitute an important source for the art and religion of a critical period of history. Perhaps they will not change our understanding of the political history of the day, but they are some of the first documents on a great cultural revolu-tion that tried to thrust back the massive force of Egyptian tradition. Scholars would like to know whether these forces, which were released at the beginning of Akh-en-Aton's reign, were the same, more violent, or more restrained than those which we know a few years later at Amarna. But what do you do with thirty thousand little blocks, this one showing the king's face, that one showing the queen's waist, a third showing the sun disk with rays, and so on?

At this point an American named Ray W. Smith appeared. He had retired from business and had become interested in the past while he formed a fine collection of ancient glass. After a few years in Egypt he knew the pressing problems. The study of the Akh-en-Aton blocks seemed to him most urgent. He conceived of the process of coding the scenes carved on the *talatat* and feeding the elements into a computer for sorting and matching.

A staff was formed in Cairo, composed chiefly of young Egyptian students of Egyptology. The *talatat* were photographed on a uniform scale. A system for coding them for the computer was devised. As an example, we might start with the most typically recurrent theme in this temple. Akh-en-Aton stands at an offering table heaped with food. Behind him stand Nefert-iti and one or two little princesses. The worship is directed toward the Aton, here shown as a sun disk with rays descending toward the offering table and the worshipers. These rays end in little hands, which may rest upon the food offerings in blessing or extend the hieroglyph for "life" to the nostrils of the king and queen. Akh-en-Aton raises empty hands in adoration to the sun disk or lifts up additional offerings.

The simplest coding for this scene starts with the sun disk and its rays. By using the branching lines of light, which are carved with mathematical precision, it is possible to record that one little block of stone shows five rays, each of which are a millimeters wide, which descend at angles of b, c, d, e, and f away from the vertical, as they branch apart. The computer may then advise that this block, which we shall here arbitrarily number 12753, has rays that may be continued on block 7654 or

11433 or 23669. Then other coded elements on the block narrow the matching down to only one other block. In any case, the advice of the computer directs the staff to pick up photographs and to use their eyes to see which of the proposed joins fits best. This emphasis on the geometric factor of slanting lines from the sun has brought to the director of the project the nickname "Sun Ray" Smith.

A *talatat* that shows an elbow may be coded in its widths and angles to match a shoulder and a hand. From the waist of the queen the computer may search for her bosom and her legs. Horses may be harnessed to their chariot. For a group of shaggy-haired foreigners the machine may be asked to look for long robes and sandals. In general, the computer has not yet learned to read hieroglyphic. Exceptions lie in names. The names of Akh-en-Aton, Nefert-iti, and the Aton are carved inside long ovals, which we call cartouches. From the upper part of one of these cartouches it is possible to code the expected lower part.

The computer is new to Egyptology, and few of the inscriptions in this temple are long enough to show recurring elements that might be coded. Nor has the machine had detailed courses in history or art. There is still a lot for an Egyptologist to do, armed with a dictionary, the publications on the tombs and temples at Amarna, a notebook, and a pencil.

Most of the money for this project has come from those same American credits in Egypt which contributed to the Nubian campaign. In Washington the Smithsonian Institution has the responsibility of supervising the allocation and expenditure of these funds for the benefit of American archaeology abroad. They scrutinize carefully the program, staff, and budget of each proposed expedition in Egypt. A committee for the Smithsonian approved the Akh-en-Aton project but asked that an Egyptologist be added to the staff. The Cairo staff did have competent scholars who were working on the problems as they arose. The routine work of sorting photographs of the *talatat*, identifying photographs made a generation ago, and matching on the basis of coding kept them too busy to do much research work in libraries. As in the case of the Hierakonpolis expedition, the request was for a known name to serve as a firmer reference. I was free and agreed to put in three months on the project.

My first love in Egypt had been Chicago House at Luxor, and I still felt most at home in the library there. Therefore the three months were divided into a short term in the Cairo office, to become closer acquainted with the material, several weeks of study in Luxor, and a final brief stretch to deliver my notes in Cairo.

The literature on this heretic king was extensive. Some of it proved to be quite immaterial to the specific purpose of understanding the temple of the *talatat*. Yet I had to do a thorough search of the literature accumulated for more than a century in case there was a brief footnote somewhere that might be pertinent. I was able to put a few anchors on my own drifting ideas. Under a high wind of criticism these anchors might still drag a little, but at least they would not stray so far.

There was the question of the scenes of jubilee so early in the king's reign. Normally such a jubilee celebrated thirty years of kingship. Why did they hold a jubilee in the first five years? Was the jubilee that of the king Akh-en-Aton or of the god, the Aton? Apparently there was a father-son identification of god and king, so that the ceremonial was for both. Perhaps also the new religion, art, architecture, and government were being confirmed by a festival of renewal, as if the revolutionary regime were actually reconfirmation. These questions have still not been answered.

Then there was the fascinating queen, Nefert-iti. Over and over again she was depicted in faithful attendance upon her husband. Was she then the quiet and dutiful wife who never budged from her lord's side and never engaged in any activity of her own? Certainly not. A full generation ago, when a French architect at Karnak was taking down the Second Pylon to rebuild it, he found inside the masonry some *talatat* that showed

Nefert-iti acting without Akh-en-Aton. She was offering to the sun god all by herself. The architect understood that these pieces came from "altars," as he called them, for the personal use of the queen. The careful work of the Cairo staff disposed of the idea that these blocks could have come from altars. In reconstruction they became square pillars about twenty feet high! No one could have placed offerings upon altars so high. The scenes on the four sides of these pillars were unique. Elsewhere in this temple or in the scenes at Amarna, Akh-en-Aton was rarely seen without Nefert-iti. Yet she appeared on this material without him. Every scene here showed the queen, followed by one or two daughters, making an offering to the Aton. Surely these blocks came from a separate place of worship for the queen, a place in which she might be attended only by her daughters.

This was unprecedented, though we knew already about parts of temples that had been dedicated to queens or princesses. The texts at Amarna told us about structures for some royal lady that were called "sun-shades of the god Re." These were small, and the scenes in the Amarna tombs showed them as different architecturally from these tall and square pillars. It would seem that a unique place of worship was built at Karnak for the exclusive use of Nefert-iti.

It was possible to go further in the study of this remarkable woman. The rays of the sun gave life only to the nostrils of the king and the queen. Nefert-iti was given a second name in a cartouche, just as kings took a ruling name when they ascended the throne. The figure of Nefert-iti was carved on the corners of stone sarcophagi, where the older religion had shown a protective goddess. And Nefert-iti was worshiped. In the Amarna tombs there were prayers to the Aton, to Akh-en-Aton, and to Nefert-iti. The conclusion was that she was treated as a goddess.

Years ago, in *The Burden of Egypt*, I questioned the finality of the monotheism of the Amarna period. Although Akh-en-Aton worshiped only the Aton, all of the courtiers worshiped

Akh-en-Aton. In his famous hymn to the Aton the king boasted that there was no one who knew the god except himself (*Ancient Near Eastern Texts*, p. 371). I wrote that there were two gods in this religion, not one. Yet there remained the possibility that, because Akh-en-Aton was the son of the Aton, the father-son relation made them parts of the same divinity. Since I had argued in *The Intellectual Adventure of Ancient Man* (pp. 62–69), that the ancient Egyptians regarded the elements of the universe as overlapping parts of a spectrum, with no sharp line of division between the human and the divine, I accepted the idea that king and god were the same. Now I found that there were three deities in the Amarna religion. It is not difficult to understand god-the-father and god-the-son. But not even recourse to the Hindu religion can persuade me to accept them as the same as god-the-daughter-in-law.

My notes on the *talatat* and related questions have clarified some of the problems of an extraordinary period of history. Perhaps it would be more accurate to say that the questions have become clearer, even if the answers may not always be persuasive to others. The notes may be of use to the people working in the Cairo office, as they attempt to match up the *talatat* on paper. However, the essential task remains a physical and pictorial one, without regard to problems of religion, art, or history.

SEVENTEEN

THE PAST
IS PROLOGUE

Ｐｅｏｐｌｅ are endlessly curious about the profession of archaeology. Is an immersion in the past an attempt to escape from today? Does a career devoted to a study of ancient times imply that antiquity was good and that the present is defective? I have given much thought to these questions, and my answer is an emphatic negative. I feel that a firm perspective on human history has value for the present day.

Perhaps one reason I enjoy studying the ancient Egyptians is that I feel some spiritual kinship with them. They have been described as lively, gay, quick to anger and to forgive, tolerant, and seeking reconciliation by compromise and adjustment. On the other hand, scholars have seen them as clinging to their past with fervor, as lacking in depth of philosophical thought or in rigor of ethical command. Although I may deplore some of the shallowness of thought or the easygoing characteristics of the ancient Egyptians, I do like the friendly accommodation they offered to apparently conflicting forces. Rigorous absolutism repels me. I have never felt happy that the prophet Samuel commanded Saul to kill all of the Amalekites, "man and woman, infant and suckling, ox and sheep, camel and ass." How could the Lord delight in the slaughter of the innocent? The ancient Egyptians would have commended Saul for sparing some of the booty. In their mythology, when the god Seth was found to be undeserving of rule, the divine council did not eliminate him. They found for him a task worthy of his talents. He was made the god of thunder in the sky. This appeals to me as a kind of enlightened therapy.

What, then, about that backward facing by the ancient Egyptians, their belief that the world order had been set up at the creation, so that it was necessary only to recapture the past instead of moving forward into a new future? Any American would reject that. But ancient anti-progressivism was a matter of dogma and not of practice, and it was modified by their tolerance of difference. The Egyptian system lasted for more than two thousand years, and it had to accept and adjust in order to survive. Like many moderns, they changed and denied that they had changed. They claimed that any new order was a return to that order which the gods had given at the beginning. So also do we Americans appeal to the principles of the Founding Fathers in order to justify the acceptance of something different.

Of course I have a nostalgia for the days and scenes of my youth, but the progressivism I learned at the family dining table when I was a boy has been too strong for me to think that the past was a golden age. At the same time we had an old New England thriftiness, which might have been rooted in the Biblical advice: "Establish the things that remain." Colloquially that became: "Don't throw out the baby with the bath water." Any nostalgia for the carefree days of boyhood has been offset by the recognition that I lived in blissful ignorance of the fact that much of the world was then suffering from disease, poverty, and oppression, without those demands for relief which are possible today. Change there must be, but I hope it can be effected with tolerance rather than violence.

Young radicals have claimed that history is irrelevant in our world of change and that it is used to preserve a bad present. That is nonsense. You cannot know where you are unless you know where you came from, and you cannot go ahead unless you know where you are. I do not want to claim too much from a knowledge of history. A minimum truth lies somewhere between Hegel's pronouncement that nations have learned nothing and have derived no governing principles from history, and Santayana's warning that those who learn nothing from the past are condemned to repeat the past. Men do not gain specific correctives for today's mistakes by studying the incidents of previous days, but they can certainly gain a better understanding of their position in time. And there is a real strengthening in the knowledge that our troubles are not unique, that man has always shown a stubborn determination to survive pain, destruction, oppression, and tragedy. Historians like Spengler and Toynbee have treated ancient Egyptian history as though it were a single lifetime, with birth, vigor, and death. I could argue that this is not true, that Egypt had a life and death under the Old Kingdom, a different life and death under the Middle Kingdom, and a third life and death under the New Kingdom. The crack of doom seemed very real, but there was a rebirth to a new and different life. Indeed, history has shown that the crack of doom is very real in terms of any culture, but that men survive and develop a new culture that has its own values. The myopic belief that the present needs no past shows a blatant ignorance.

That the present has a very different surface is undeniable. The social and technological revolution in this century has been a dizzying experience. Sixty years ago the motive power on farms lay in the muscles of men, horses, mules, and oxen. In the kitchens the never-ending bustle of women was necessary to keep the family going. There was travel by railroad or ship, but most people used their legs or the legs of horses to go places.

There were no radios or television sets, few telephones, and the newspapers concentrated on local happenings. Places like Moscow, Cairo, or Peking were too remote to cause anxiety. Except for those poor women in the kitchen, the pace was relatively relaxed.

That system of a reliance upon muscle power and of an unconcern for affairs in the outer world came down to us over thousands of years. It was codified in ancient Egypt and Babylonia as essential to civilized life. The Renaissance and the American and French Revolutions questioned basic political and economic assumptions without really changing the daily way of life.

Our present revolution in power and communications is exploding within only a few generations. Thousands of years ago a comparable revolution, the transition to agriculture, took millennia to unfold. Six thousand years ago the revolution to civilized urban life evolved over several centuries. Within this present bewildering convulsion there are values from the past that must be retained. They are not the privileges of power and wealth. They are social values. They permit and control orderly relations between men, and that is necessary for any kind of culture.

This may seem to put me on the side of those who cry out for law and order and who condemn the young people who are using forcible protest to seek a new world tomorrow. But as I look back over the centuries and contrast the present with the past, I agree with those young people that we are in a revolution and must adjust to it. Anyone who studies ancient Egypt or Greece or Elizabethan England must acknowledge that the clock cannot be turned back. A sun dial will not fit our modern need for precision. Joel said: "Your old men shall dream dreams, your young men shall see visions." Dreams are usually dreams of the past for the old: visions have a chance of becoming the future.

As an ancient historian, I would like to see a little of that old Egyptian tolerance. It would be good to accommodate to change without violence and without disrupting the rights of others. It would even be good to find a little honest enjoyment in the adventure of charting the future, a little of that ancient gaiety. Those who are sallying forth to conquer the world should march proudly with the bugles blowing and a rollicking song. Why, then, are there so many glum faces going to the high conquest? Four thousand years ago an Egyptian prophet bemoaned a collapse of civilization with the words: "Men laugh with the laughter of sickness, and there is no one who weeps because of death. . . . A man's heart pursues himself alone" (*Ancient Near Eastern Texts*).

The supreme Egyptian virtue lay in something they called *ma'at*, which we translate variously as "right, right-doing, justice, truth, evenness, order, balance." This was a social value, because it applied to relations between man and man, man and ruler, ruler and those who were ruled, and between man and god. That which demands respect and order between persons still seems a useful value.

BIOGRAPHICAL NOTES
HONORS AND AWARDS
INDEX

BIOGRAPHICAL NOTES

Allen, T. George (1885–1969), American Egyptologist, one of Breasted's students; specialist on the Book of the Dead; editorial secretary of the Oriental Institute, 1927–50.

Atiya, Aziz S. (1898–), Egyptian specialist in Arabic and medieval history; director of the Middle East Center at the University of Utah, 1961–67.

Baer, Klaus (1930–), Ph.D. at Chicago; Professor of Egyptology at the University of Chicago since 1965.

Bliss, Daniel (1898–), clergyman of the United Church of Christ; brought up in Beirut, grandson of the founder of the American University there; active for American colleges in Lebanon and for Arab refugees.

Borchardt, Ludwig (1863–1938), a leading German field archaeologist and scientist; discoverer of the bust of Nefert-iti at Amarna in 1912.

Braidwood, Robert J. (1907–), archaeologist specializing in the prehistory of the Fertile Crescent; Professor of Old World Prehistory at the University of Chicago since 1954.

Breasted, James H. (1865–1935), of the University of Chicago;

leading American historian of the ancient world, philologist, and outstanding teacher.

Brew, J. O. (1906–), Peabody Professor of Archaeology and Ethnology at Harvard; director of the Peabody Museum; chairman of the UNESCO Committee for Monuments.

Brown, W. Norman (1892–), professor of Sanskrit at the University of Pennsylvania; presiding officer at the 27th International Congress of Orientalists at Ann Arbor in 1967.

Bunche, Ralph J. (1904–), specialist on colonial problems; awarded the Nobel Peace Prize in 1950 for securing adjustments between Israel and the Arab states; undersecretary general of the United Nations 1968–1971.

Cameron, George G. (1905–), specialist in early Iranian history; left the University of Chicago in 1948 to head the Department of Near Eastern Languages and Literatures at the University of Michigan.

Capps, Edward (1866–1950), taught Classics at Princeton, 1907–1936; American minister to Greece, 1920–21.

Carter, Howard (1873–1939), British artist and archaeologist; discoverer of the tomb of Tut-ankh-Amon in 1922.

Chiera, Edward (1885–1933), Italian-born Assyriologist; excavator in Iraq; editor of the *Assyrian Dictionary* at the Oriental Institute from 1927.

Conklin, Edwin Grant (1863–1952), taught biology at Princeton, 1908–1936; influential in revitalizing the American Philosophical Society.

Davies, Norman de Garis (1865–1941), of Great Britain, formed with his wife Nina the ablest copying team for Egyptian tombs.

de Buck, Adriaan (1892–1959), Dutch, professor of Egyptology at the University of Leiden.

Delougaz, Pinhas Pierre (1901–), Russian-born excavator in Iraq, Israel, and Iran; professor of Archaeology, University of Chicago, 1960–67, then at the University of California at Los Angeles.

Dodge, Bayard (1888–), specialist in Arabic literature; president of the American University of Beirut, 1923–48.

Driver, Godfrey R. (1892–), of Great Britain, professor of Semitic Philology at Oxford University from 1938.

Eddy, William A. (1896–1962), professor of English, president of

Hobart and William Smith Colleges, 1936–42; minister to Saudi Arabia, 1944–46.

Edgerton, William F. (1893–1970), one of Breasted's students; professor of Egyptology at the University of Chicago from 1929; specialist in demotic and the history of the Egyptian language.

Erman, Adolf (1854–1937), German, professor of Egyptology at the University of Berlin; grammarian, philologist, and teacher.

Fairbank, John K. (1907–), Higginson Professor of Chinese History and director of the East Asia Research Center at Harvard since 1959.

Fairservis, Walter A., Jr. (1921–), excavator in Afghanistan, India, and Egypt; now at Vassar College and the Museum of Natural History in New York.

Frankfort, Henri (1897–1954), Dutch-born excavator in Egypt and Iraq; professor of Archaeology at Chicago 1939–40; director of the Warburg Institute in London from 1949.

Gardiner, Sir Alan Henderson (1879–1963), British philologist and translator; author of the most influential Egyptian grammar (1927); knighted in 1948.

Giddings, Franklin H. (1855–1931), born in Sherman, Connecticut; first professor of a named chair in sociology at Columbia, 1894–1928.

Griffith, Francis Ll. (1862–1934), of Great Britain, set on a sound basis the study of demotic about 1909.

Hall, Clifton Rumery (1884–1945), professor of American History at Princeton University.

Hall, Walter Phelps (1884–1962), professor of European History (the nineteenth century) at Princeton University.

Harper, George M., Jr. (1899–), retired in 1970 as professor of Greek and Latin at Williams College.

Hartshorne, Richard (1899–), retired in 1970 as professor of Geography at the University of Wisconsin.

Hayes, William C. (1903–1963), Egyptologist, philologist, and historian; curator of Egyptian Art at the Metropolitan Museum in New York.

Hitti, Philip K. (1886–), Lebanese-born professor of Semitic Literature at Princeton, 1926–54; historian of the Arabs; architect of an outstanding department at Princeton.

Irwin, William A. (1884–1967), Canadian, professor of Old Testament at the University of Chicago, 1930–50.

Jacobsen, Thorkild (1904–), Danish-born specialist in the Sumerian phase of cuneiform writing; with the Oriental Institute from 1929, its director, 1946–48; at Harvard University since 1962.

Junker, Hermann (1877–1962), Austrian philologist and excavator in Egypt.

Klasens, Adolf (1917–), Dutch excavator in Egypt; curator of the Museum of Antiquities in Leiden.

Kraeling, Carl H. (1897–1966), specialist on the Hellenistic Orient; taught at Yale, 1938–50; director of the Oriental Institute 1950–60.

Lacau, Pierre (1873–1963), French linguist; director-general of the Egyptian Antiquities Service, 1914–35.

Langer, William L. (1896–), Coolidge Professor of History at Harvard, 1936–64.

Lauer, Jean-Philippe (1902–), French excavator; restorer of the Stepped Pyramid at Saqqarah.

Lee, Rensselaer W. (1898–), retired in 1966 as Marquand Professor of Art and Archaeology and chairman of department at Princeton.

Lloyd, Seton (1902–), British excavator in Egypt, Iraq, and Turkey; author of paperbacks on Near Eastern archaeology.

Loud, Gordon (1900–1971), excavator for the Oriental Institute, 1929–41, at Khorsabad (Iraq) and Megiddo (Palestine).

Luckenbill, D. D. (1881–1927), professor of Assyriology; first editor of the Oriental Institute's *Assyrian Dictionary*.

Mallowan, Sir Max (1904–), British excavator at Nineveh and other sites in northern Iraq and Syria; knighted in 1968.

Maspero, Gaston (1846–1916), French historian, philologist, and influential Egyptologist; director-general of the Egyptian Antiquities Service for more than twenty years.

McEwan Calvin W. (1906–1950), directed Oriental Institute excavations in northern Syria.

Michalowski, Kazimierz (1901–), Polish Egyptologist; excavator in Egypt, the Sudan, Syria, and Cyprus.

Mond, Sir Robert (1867–1938), British industrial chemist; patron of excavations at Thebes and Armant.

Biographical Notes

Munro, Dana Carleton (1886–1933), taught medieval history at Princeton.

Nelson, Harold H. (1878–1954), one of Breasted's students; teacher of history and English at the American University of Beirut, 1904–1924; director of the Oriental Institute's Epigraphic Survey at Luxor, 1924–47.

Noblecourt, Christiane Desroches- (1913–), French specialist in Egyptian art; curator at the Louvre Museum; formed the Center of Documentation in Cairo.

Oppenheim, A. Leo (1904–), Austrian-born professor of Assyriology at the University of Chicago; first holder of the John A. Wilson Professorship in Oriental Studies; editor-in-chief of the *Assyrian Dictionary* since 1954; author of books on ancient Mesopotamia.

Petrie, Sir Flinders (1853–1942), British excavator; father of scientific archaeology; knighted in 1923.

Piotrovski, Boris Borisovitch (1908–), Russian archaeologist; connected with the Hermitage in Leningrad; excavator in Soviet Armenia.

Price, Ira M. (1856–1939), cuneiformist and teacher of Old Testament at the University of Chicago, 1893–1925.

Pritchard, James B. (1909–), excavator in Palestine and Jordan; professor of Religious Thought at the University of Pennsylvania since 1962.

Rainey, Froelich (1907–), anthropologist; director of the University Museum, Philadelphia since 1947.

Rauschenbusch Walter (1861–1918), American clergyman; speaker and writer on the social gospel.

Read, Conyers (1881–1959), professor of English History at the University of Pennsylvania, 1934–1951.

Redfield, Robert (1897–1959), social anthropologist at the University of Chicago; field work in Central America.

Reisner, George A. (1867–1942), Egyptologist; excavator in Egypt and the Sudan; professor, Harvard University; curator, Egyptian Department, Boston Museum of Fine Arts.

Riis, Jacob A. (1849–1914), Danish-born American journalist and social worker.

Rostovtzev, Mikhail I. (1870–1952), Russian-born historian of the

Greco-Roman Orient; excavator at Dura-Europos on the Euphrates; taught at Yale.

Sandford, Kenneth S. (1899–), British geologist and prehistorian; director of the Oriental Institute's Prehistoric Survey along the Nile, 1926–33.

Schaefer, J. Heinrich (1868–1957), German, curator of Egyptian antiquities at the Berlin Museum.

Scharff, Alexander (1892–1950), German philologist and archaeologist; professor of Egyptology at the University of Munich.

Seele, Keith C. (1898–1971), one of Kurt Sethe's students at Berlin; taught at the University of Chicago, 1936–64; headed the Oriental Institute excavations in Nubia, 1960–64.

Sethe, Kurt (1869–1934), German linguist; professor of Egyptology at the University of Berlin, succeeding Erman.

Smith, Ray W. (1897–), American businessman and government official; director of the American Research Center in Egypt, 1963–65; then director of the Akhenaten Temple Project for the University of Pennsylvania.

Smith, William Stevenson (1907–1969), curator of Egyptian Art at the Boston Museum of Fine Arts.

Spiegelberg, Wilhelm (1870–1930), German specialist in demotic; professor of Egyptology at the University of Munich.

Sprengling, Martin (1877–1959), professor of Arabic and Islamic History at the University of Chicago, 1915–43.

Steindorff, Georg (1861–1951), of Germany and then the United States; professor of Egyptology at the University of Leipzig; excavator; editor of Baedeker's *Egypt and the Sudan*.

Winlock, Herbert E. (1884–1950), of the Metropolitan Museum of Art in New York; excavator, chiefly in western Thebes.

Wright, Walter L., Jr. (1900–1949), president of Robert College, Istanbul, 1935–44; professor of Turkish Language and History at Princeton University.

HONORS AND AWARDS

1937   Corresponding Member, German Archaeological Institute
1938   Earl Lecturer, University of California
1944- President, American Oriental Society
 1945
1948   Fogg Lecturer, Archaeological Institute of America
1952   Corresponding Member, Commission for a UNESCO Cultural History of Mankind
1952- Fulbright Lecturer, Universities of Alexandria and Cairo
 1953
1953   Appointed Andrew MacLeish Distinguished Service Professor of Egyptology, University of Chicago
1954   Member, American Philosophical Society
1957   Named by Loyola University as one of One Hundred Distinguished Chicagoans
1960- Member and Rapporteur, UNESCO Consultative Committee
 1965 to the United Arab Republic for the Salvage of the Nubian Monuments; acting chairman, 1964
1961   Honorary Doctor of Letters, Princeton University

1965- Member, Group of Archaeologists and Landscape Architects
1971 for the Salvage of Abu Simbel

1968 John A. Wilson Professorship of Oriental Studies established
at the University of Chicago

John A. Wilson annual prize for an essay in archaeology
established by the students' Archaeology Club, University
of Chicago

Member, American Academy of Arts and Sciences

1968- Councillor, American Philosophical Society
1971

1969 September 12, *Studies in Honor of John A. Wilson* presented
by colleagues and former students in honor of seventieth
birthday

Corresponding Member, Institut d'Égypte

1970 de Buck Memorial Lecturer, University of Leiden

INDEX

Index